WOMEN, POLIT
THE PUBLIC S

Ann Brooks

First published in Great Britain in 2019 by

Policy Press
University of Bristol
1-9 Old Park Hill
Bristol
BS2 8BB
UK
t: +44 (0)117 954 5940
pp-info@bristol.ac.uk
www.policypress.co.uk

North America office:
Policy Press
c/o The University of Chicago Press
1427 East 60th Street
Chicago, IL 60637, USA
t: +1 773 702 7700
f: +1 773-702-9756
sales@press.uchicago.edu
www.press.uchicago.edu

British Library Cataloguing in Publication Data
A catalogue record for this book is available from the British Library

Library of Congress Cataloging-in-Publication Data
A catalog record for this book has been requested

978-1-4473-3063-9 hardback
978-1-4473-4135-2 paperback
978-1-4473-4113-0 ePdf
978-1-4473-4137-6 ePub
978-1-4473-4136-9 Mobi

Cover design by Andrew Corbett
Front cover image: Getty
Printed and bound in Great Britain by CMP, Poole
Policy Press uses environmentally responsible print partners

Contents

About the author

Ann Brooks is a Visiting Professor at the Australian Catholic University (Sydney), at the Institute of Religion, Politics and Society in 2018–19. She is a Fellow of the Academy of Social Sciences (FAcSS) and has held senior academic positions in universities in Australia, Singapore and the UK. Most recently she was Professor of Sociology at Bournemouth University, prior to which she was also Professor of Sociology and Cultural Studies and Head of School of Social Sciences at Adelaide University (2008–11). She has also held research fellowships at the University of California, Berkeley (2011–13) and the Asia Research Institute at the National University of Singapore (2013–14). Ann has been an International Research Investigator with the Australia Research Council-funded Centre of Excellence for the History of Emotions 2011–18 in Australia. She is author of *Academic Women* (Open University Press, 1997); *Postfeminisms: Feminism, Cultural Theory and Cultural Forms* (Routledge, 1997); *Gender and the Restructured University* (Open University Press, 2001); *Gendered Work in Asian Cities: The New Economy and Changing Labour Markets* (Ashgate, 2006); *Social Theory in Contemporary Asia* (Routledge, 2010); *Gender, Emotions and Labour Markets: Asian and Western Perspectives* (Routledge, 2013); *Emotions in Transmigration: Transformation, Movement and Identity* (Palgrave, 2012) (with Ruth Simpson); *Popular Culture, Global Intercultural Perspectives* (Palgrave, 2014); *Consumption, Rights and States – Comparing Global Cities in Asia and the US* (Anthem Press, 2014) (with Lionel Wee); and *Emotions and Social Change: Historical and Sociological Perspectives* (Routledge, New York, 2014) (co-edited with David Lemmings). Her latest book with Routledge is *Genealogies of Emotions, Intimacy and Desire: Theories of Changes in Emotional Regimes from Medieval Society to Late Modernity* (Routledge New York, 2017). Ann's forthcoming book is *Love and Intimacy in Contemporary Society* (Routledge, 2019).

Acknowledgements

I wish to acknowledge the support of a number of people and institutions in the publication of this book. My thanks to Professor Bryan Turner, Director of the Institute of Religion, Politics and Society at Australian Catholic University and to Australian Catholic University for the invitation to be a Visiting Professor in 2018–19. I completed the book in Sydney in an intellectually vibrant environment. I wish to acknowledge the support of the Australia Research Council's Centre of Excellence for the History of Emotions during the period 2011–18, which supported the development of this book by providing funding for me to undertake research at the Huntington Library in Pasadena, California in 2016 and 2017. My particular thanks to Katrina Tap and Tanya Tuffey for facilitating this. My thanks to my excellent editor Victoria Pittman, Jo Morton and Shannon Kneis at Policy Press/ Bristol University Press and the entire team for their help in preparing the book for publication.

Professor Ann Brooks
Sydney, 2019

Introduction

Women, Politics and the Public Sphere explores the relationship between women, political discourse and political representation historically, contemporaneously and cross-culturally. The focus is historically in the United Kingdom (UK) and contemporaneously in the United States (US). The monograph hypothesizes the legacy of 18th-century intellectual groupings that were dominated by women such as members of the 'bluestocking circles' and other more radical intellectual and philosophical thinkers such as Catherine Macaulay and Mary Wollstonecraft. These individuals and groups that emerged in the 18th century established 'intellectual spaces' for the emergence of women public intellectuals in subsequent centuries.

While the bluestockings were formed by affluent and educated women, other more radical thinkers such as Macaulay and Wollstonecraft were not part of the bluestockings and had very different backgrounds socially and economically. Wollstonecraft and Macaulay had a significant impact on the emergence of women as leading public and political figures in later centuries. These groupings and individuals established a basis for the emergence of a range of social, political and literary movements such as the Bloomsbury Group, the suffrage movement and, latterly, feminism as a social and political movement as well as the civil rights movement.

This monograph is not meant to be a detailed and chronological historical analysis of the emergence of women within political representation, but intellectually it traces the legacy of 18th-century women thinkers, writers and political philosophers in understanding the emergence of women public intellectuals in the UK and the US. The kind of legacy established in the chapters of this book can be seen in considering the radical republican politics of Catherine Macaulay, as compared with the politics of a key Republican woman public intellectual in the US, Condoleezza Rice. The challenges posed to the conventional gender politics and normative structures by Wollstonecraft and Macaulay can be compared in political terms with the liberal equal opportunities feminism in the writings of politically active individuals such as Hillary Clinton and Sheryl Sandberg. Macaulay was more radical politically than Wollstonecraft. Both Wollstonecraft and Macaulay led more radical personal lives. The book focuses on the success of women public intellectuals in the US, as there is a much clearer pattern of women moving from high-level academic positions into different US administrations. This is different from the UK, where women have to be elected into positions where they can articulate policy. In the US prominent women academics have already established a profile, mainly in academic life but also in the corporate sphere, before they are invited to join an administration. As can be seen from the profile of many of the women discussed, they have significant academic profiles and are recognized for the contribution made in academic life. There is far less in the way of women with established academic profiles moving into public life in the UK, and this is partly to do with the narrow definition of academic life in the UK limiting the opportunities for women, should they want to move into public life in politics. As a result the academic pedigree of women in politics in the UK is less prominent or impressive.

The book is about the fault-lines established in the 18th-century for later developments in social and political discourse for women politically.

Aims and objectives

The aims of the monograph are to trace the patterns of educated women writers, philosophers and contributors to social and political discourse who provided openings that later women public intellectuals could occupy, and to understand the differences of emphasis and focus in their position over time. The objectives of the book are: firstly, to understand the emergence of women as public intellectuals in the 18th century, particularly through the influence of radical women thinkers such as Macaulay and Wollstonecraft as well as more moderate but learned groupings such as the bluestockings and their engagement with international political and public discourse; secondly, to consider the impact of these early movements for women's involvement in politics, education and other spheres of public life; thirdly, to trace the emergence of contemporary women public intellectuals in the US and their representation in contemporary political and social life.

Methodological/archival issues and research

The monograph draws on primary archival research undertaken during 2016 and 2017 in the Huntington Library in San Marino, Pasadena, Southern California, which has a rich collection of historical and literary materials, letters and manuscripts on the bluestocking circles and some of their leading figures, including Elizabeth Montagu. The research was funded by the Australia Research Council (ARC) Centre of Excellence for the History of Emotions 2011–2018, and with a smaller grant from Seed Corn Funding from Bournemouth University. The availability and extent of the archival materials is unmatched globally and has provided invaluable resources for this book.

Reviewers of the book proposal and for allied research have been very helpful in refining the original scope of the research. They highlighted a need to focus on and consider a reconsideration of feminism in late modernity linked to women as public intellectuals, and a greater emphasis on contemporary women public intellectuals in relation to political representation. This is reflected in the wide range of feminist thinkers and commentators in the chapters of the book. The focus is on a more original approach to this as opposed to a focus on feminist theoretical debates that have been written about elsewhere (for a consideration of feminist theory and late modernity see Brooks, 2008, 2014; Brooks and Wee, 2008, 2012). The chapters of the book are outlined below.

Chapter One: The gender politics of 'bluestocking philosophy'

The bluestocking has traditionally been defined as a scholarly or intellectual woman and 'bluestocking circles' assembled in the homes of a number of affluent and educated women in the 18th century who cultivated social discourse among women and men. Eger and Peltz (2008: i) comment that: 'The initial cultivation of "bluestocking philosophy", in this mixed company, may be seen as the social expression of an Enlightenment belief in freedom of enquiry irrespective of nature or gender.' In addition, 'bluestocking circles' including Elizabeth Montagu, known as the 'Queen of the Blues', helped to forge a public identity for women public intellectuals through Montagu's own scholarship as well as her support for other women writers.

The early 'bluestocking circles' were not established as a vehicle for promoting equity or women's rights, or even rights of citizenship (Lefebvre and White, 2010). However, they played an important role in the second half of the 18th century in entrenching cultural and social transformation into the social system. In addition they 'played a crucial role in a widening and defining of women's social roles in the eighteenth century' (Pohl and Schellenberg, 2003: 3). The early bluestocking circles have been defined by Kelly (1999a) as essentially 'a progressive-aristocratic' programme with the key characteristics being class and property. They opened up debates around conceptions of 'civic virtue' (Lefebvre and White, 2010) as well as political power (Hill, 1992, 1995).

Elizabeth Montagu was a central figure in the development of 'bluestocking circles' and, along with Elizabeth Vesey and Frances Boscawen, they were 'wealthy women who invented a new kind of informal sociability and nurtured a sense of intellectual community' (Eger, 2008: 21). Montagu epitomizes what Guest (2003: 59) defines as the political character of 'Bluestocking Feminism', which she describes as 'a conservative group – conservative in their political inclinations as well as in their attitudes to class and to sexuality'. Clear examples of this can be seen in the extensive collection of letters sent by Elizabeth Montagu (1825, 1974) to members of the 'Bluestocking Circle' including Elizabeth Carter. Both Montagu and Carter engaged with classical and literary scholars in their writings and thus established a pattern of women's commentary on significant literary and philosophical debates and figures.

Eger (2008: 32) notes that 'Montagu used the phrase "Bluestocking College" which conveys the sense in which the circle invested in the idea of education at a time when women were denied access to university'. Montagu also mentored a number of women writers, including Hester Chapone (1773). She also granted annuities to fellow authors, including Elizabeth Carter, Hester Chapone and Sarah Fielding. She was recognized as mentoring women and for promoting the arts, but she was also seen as patronizing towards less wealthy women and having a rigidity of outlook as well as being moralizing towards the second marriages to younger men of Catherine Macaulay and Mary Wollstonecraft.

Chapter Two: Gender and the politics of the public sphere

The bluestockings were instrumental in framing a set of literary and political discourses that opened the door for a range of political movements where women occupied leading positions, including the Bloomsbury Group and the suffrage movement. The understanding of the bourgeois public sphere originates with Habermas (1989: 55–6). He interestingly distinguishes in his work between two forms of public sphere: the first is the world of letters. In this form of public sphere, Habermas described 'privatized individuals in their capacity as human beings [who] communicated through critical debate'. Secondly, Habermas identifies the 'political realm', which he describes as 'private people in their capacity as owners of commodities [who] communicated through rational-critical debate'.

Guest (2003: 65) links Habermas's work with members of the bluestockings including Hannah More, and shows that an educated elite had emerged by the late 18th century which incorporated a social world including women and men. Guest insightfully observes that the notion of an educated elite was not restricted to the bluestockings and 'constituted something resembling Habermas's notion of the literary public formed by the educated class'.

Guest's assessment of the relationship between gender and politics is interesting as, despite the significance of women writers within the public sphere through elite groupings such as the bluestockings, their role was still limited. As Guest (2003: 78) illustrates, while the bluestockings were actively involved in literary and political debates their distance from the political sphere highlights the gendered character of the 18th-century public sphere. While Guest shows that Habermas offers the potential of a feminine political voice, in terms of political involvement, it is the juxtaposition of 'Habermas's public world of letters' to the political realm which establishes their distance. Guest does note, however – and this is an argument developed in the book – that the kind of discourse engaged in by the bluestockings encouraged the voices of more politically radical writers such as Macaulay and Wollstonecraft across a range of subjects, including gender.

Chapter Three: 'Uncompromising politics': Mary Wollstonecraft and Catherine Macaulay

Two of the most interesting and political women writing in the 18th century were Catherine Macaulay and Mary Wollstonecraft. Hill (1992) describes Macaulay (but it could also apply to Wollstonecraft) as 'a woman in a man's world, unorthodox and [an] anti-establishment figure' (Hill, 1992: 130).

Both were instrumental in the development of feminist political thought and Guest (2003: 61) maintains that by the 1790s 'Catherine Macaulay and Mary Wollstonecraft had achieved a kind of political articulacy and a degree of public audibility that are central to the emergence of modern feminist politics in Britain'. This was not seen as an area that women should comment on. Both Macaulay and Wollstonecraft showed that women as public intellectuals could defend republican political principles.

In addition, both contributed to debates on education and both believed in the same education for women and men. However, Macaulay was less concerned with the position of women in society than Wollstonecraft was. Elsewhere Hill (1995) shows that they were close on issues of democracy, equality and women's rights. Both were concerned with the education of women and children. On the issue of suffrage, Macaulay was in favour of full male suffrage but did not raise the question of women's suffrage.

Both also shared with many in 'bluestocking circles' reservations about 'lower class women', assuming political rights as being in practice restricted to women of the 'propertied classes' (Hill, 1995: 185). This view of women's rights was not untypical of how they were understood by 18th-century radicals. Macaulay and Wollstonecraft held the same view as others who were 'not prepared to extend the suffrage to women because they regarded women as incapable of exercising a free, rational and independent choice' (Todd and Butler, 1989: 21, cited in Hill, 1995: 186).

Wollstonecraft's (1792) *A Vindication of the Rights of Woman* and Macaulay's (1790a) *Letters on Education* are both critical of educating women to make them 'more attractive for men', but Wollstonecraft goes further than Macaulay in arguing that the education of women should be about giving them more independence. Similarly, Wollstonecraft maintained that women should work and become independent (as she herself had done). Porter (2004) locates Wollstonecraft's feminism in a general trend towards sexual liberation and acknowledges Wollstonecraft and her husband, William Godwin, as 'the Enlightenment's premier husband and wife team'.

Chapter Four: Women writers: setting the terms of the debate

Many of the bluestockings were published writers: Montagu (1769) published *An Essay on the Writings and Genius of Shakespear*, and her sister Sarah Scott (1762) wrote a *Description of Millenium Hall and the Country Adjacent*. Other published bluestocking works were Elizabeth Carter's (1758) *All the Works of Epictetus*, Hannah More's (1786) *The Bas Bleu*, Hester Chapone's (1773) *Letters on the Improvement of the Mind*, and Eliza Haywood's (1744) periodical *The Female Spectator*. Eger (2008: 48) notes that 'Haywood's periodical covered a wide range of subjects including politics, science, fashion, literary criticism and social analysis (especially of courtship and marriage), and conjured up a group of intelligent, engaged women as contributors, readers and discussants.' Eger also notes that Montagu and Carter showed that women could succeed in areas traditionally defined as areas where men excelled. Montagu was celebrated as a woman writer who challenged Voltaire's notorious criticism of Shakespeare.

Macaulay's *History of England*, in eight volumes, was recognized by key political figures such as Benjamin Franklin, who bought the eight volumes and included it in the University of Virginia library. Wollstonecraft's (1792) *A Vindication of the Rights of Woman* made explicit claims for the rights of women to full citizenship and became a central commentary and early feminist treatise on women's rights.

Regardless of the success of these women writers, and probably as a result of it, at the start of the 19th century the combined social and intellectual prominence of so many intelligent women was responded to with both resentment and disgust by many men. An example of how men patronized and demeaned women is shown in the lithograph by the Irish painter Daniel Maclise entitled *Regina's Maid of Honour* where he domesticates intellectual women in order to make them more palatable, while at the same time belittling their achievements. As Eger (2008: 132) shows:

> His subjects are ...: Anna Maria Hall (1800–81), Irish novelist and children's writer; Letitia Elizabeth Landon (1802–38), known as L.E.L, the best-selling and innovative poet; Lady Sydney Morgan (1783–1859), novelist and Irish nationalist, author of the famous *Wild Irish Girl* (1806); Harriet Martineau (1802–7), essayist, popular educator and political economist; Jane Porter (1776–1850) whose novel about Scottish independence ... was highly popular ...; Caroline Norton (1808–77) poet, novelist and pamphleteer; and finally, ... Marguerite, Countess of Blessington (1789–1849), novelist, journalist and literary hostess.

The establishment of a recognized and significant presence of women in the 'world of letters' paved the way for a wide range of social and political commentary from women writers such as Jane Austen, George Eliot and, later, Virginia Woolf. As Eger (2008: 134) comments for this reason: 'the novel, a genre traditionally associated with the feminine, provided an important intellectual outlet ... Historically the novel has provided an important cultural space in which the place of women in society can be explored, challenged and developed. It has also allowed women to investigate important questions of female cultural tradition and legacy that the bluestockings first established as integral to their identity as professional women and artists.' As Eger (2008: 136) also notes, 20th-century novelists continued this tradition, such as 'Jean Rhys [who] wrote a prequel to *Jane Eyre* entitled *Wide Sargasso Sea* (1966) in which she described the painful story of the first Mrs Rochester, connecting Bronte's female oppression with an analysis of racial oppression in the nineteenth-century British Empire.'

In addition, despite significant differences between writers such as Wollstonecraft and Eliot, with Eliot openly critical of Wollstonecraft's *Vindication of the Rights of Woman*, there were areas where they shared similarities in life-style and in their commitment to education. Eliot, like Wollstonecraft lived openly with a man without being married; she was also committed to women's education and was influenced by Barbara Leigh Bodichon, who was involved with Emily Davies in the establishment of Girton College in Cambridge.

The Bloomsbury Group can be seen to be in the direct tradition of the Bluestocking Circle, and was characterized by a circle of intellectuals including Virginia Woolf and Vanessa Bell. Woolf, like Wollstonecraft, saw economic independence as crucial in defining women's independence.

Pohl and Schellenberg (2003: 7) maintain that the '"bluestockings" occupied a contradictory position within the discourses of eighteenth-century femininity'. The kind of criticism levelled at them, particularly from conservative critics, became 'a proxy in ideological disputes conservatives and liberals' (Pohl and Schellenberg, 2003: 6). While the bluestockings (with the exception of Wollstonecraft) could not be seen as providing any direct legacy for feminism, Eger (2008: 127) argues that this has to be set in the context of the backlash against intellectual women in the 19th century, when she claims that they acquired their most negative and misogynist connotations. Significant figures in the literary and cultural establishment launched vitriolic attacks on the bluestockings. The Romantics were particularly prominent in this regard. In the tradition of Walpole and Burke's critique of radical women writers of the 1790s, poets, writers and critics launched vicious attacks on women writers.

Chapter Five: The role of social movements leading to the emergence of women public intellectuals

This chapter traces the impact of social movements in the establishment of women public intellectuals, including the period of the pre-social movement phase, which forms the first part of the chapter. The second part of the chapter focuses on the significance of social movements, including the suffrage movement, the feminist movement and the civil rights movement, in leading to the emergence of women as public intellectuals. The chapter highlights how social movements have accelerated the progression of women into roles as public intellectuals;

and how also the fields in which women appear have also expanded exponentially.

This chapter considers the legacy of the bluestockings in the context of the role of social movements: in feminist thinking, in civil rights and in terms of the social and cultural diversity that dominated the 20th century. Parallels will be drawn between the diversity of thinking among the bluestockings – from the republican politics of Macaulay, to the equal opportunities philosophy of Mary Wollstonecraft, to the conservatism of Montagu and Carter and to the connections between the personal and political, as shown in the lives of Wollstonecraft, Macaulay and others who were scorned because of their second marriages to younger men. Parallels will be drawn to different branches of feminism and how feminism has taken forward many of the issues raised by these women.

Chapters Six and Seven: Contemporary women public intellectuals: the United States (1) and (2)

The final two chapters of the book focus on how women public intellectuals now reflect much more social and cultural diversity and come from a wide range of social, political and cultural contexts. I focus on the US, as American women public intellectuals have made much more significant inroads into political representation. The US, it is true, has not yet elected a woman president, and the UK has had two women prime ministers. However, this is the result of narrow political election within political parties as opposed to nationwide election, as in the US. Additionally, women public intellectuals in the US who have served in different administrations have already established themselves as prominent in academic life.

A wide range of women public intellectuals in the US will be drawn on to highlight the parallels with some of the bluestocking thinkers and philosophy. The radical republican politics of Catherine Macaulay is compared with the politics of a key Republican woman public intellectual, Condoleezza Rice; the challenges to women's rights as human rights highlighted by Mary Wollstonecraft and the equal opportunities feminism of Wollstonecraft are reflected in the writings and ideas of Hillary Clinton, Anne-Marie Slaughter, Sheryl Sandberg and others.

Contemporary US women public intellectuals will be the focus of these chapters and will show the transition they have made from their position as high-flying academic public intellectuals to serving in different capacities for different administrations. They include, among others: Anne-Marie Slaughter (Princeton University), Samantha Power (Harvard University), Condoleezza Rice (Stanford University), Sheryl Sandberg (Harvard University), Elizabeth Warren (Harvard University, Brookings Institution and Yale), Susan Rice (Stanford, Brookings Institution) and Hillary Clinton (Wellesley).

In each case I have reflected on how the issues of race and class as well as gender have impacted on the positions they have held within different political administrations. Most come from what the US calls 'the progressive' end of politics, and clearly their support for issues linked to women's rights is part of this. In considering the significance of these women and their legacy and contribution to US politics and society, we might consider what we might learn in the UK for a similar pattern of success for women public intellectuals.

ONE

The gender politics of 'bluestocking philosophy'

Introduction

The idea of a single, unified conceptualization of what constituted a bluestocking and what was understood as a bluestocking philosophy is somewhat misleading, as the idea of a single voice emerging from this group is almost a contradiction in terms. What can be identified is who made up the bluestocking circles and what they aspired to be and to do. The idea of a group of like-minded educated women forming intellectual groupings where life beyond the private and domestic was the source of interest and discussion was certainly a break with a normative structure where the idea of a rationally based Enlightenment discourse was seen as the domain of men – and indeed, educated male philosophers, and social and literary commentators. The term 'bluestocking' originally applied to women and men and, as Eger and Peltz (2008: 1) show, the idea of a 'bluestocking philosophy' was something that applied to a mixed company and was seen as 'social expression of an Enlightenment belied in freedom of enquiry'.

As Pohl and Schellenberg (2003: 2) comment of the bluestocking gatherings:

> These informal gatherings united men and women primarily of the gentry and upper classes, with the participation of a number of more middle-class professionals, in the pursuit of intellectual improvement, polite sociability, the refinement of the arts through patronage, ... The Bluestocking women can be seen to have played a central role in the cultural and social transformations of the second half of the century that entrenched this system of values in England.

The bluestocking circles started to meet in the 1750s and appear to have been at least in part modelled on the French salonnières and were dedicated to 'rational conversation' (Montagu, 1765, cited in Pohl and Schellenberg, 2003). They formed around affluent, educated, conservative, prominent hostesses who were friends, including Elizabeth Montagu, Elizabeth Vesey, Frances Boscawen and Elizabeth Carter, who were avid correspondents and united in what they saw as the 'bluestocking doctrine' of rational conversation and debate.

Eger and Peltz (2008: 1) show that they largely met in the homes of Montagu, Vesey and Boscawen, who were regarded as innovative women who established salon-like discussions that provided a platform for women to have a voice. However, they also note that while the groups were primarily women they did include a range of male literary and philosophical scholars, including Edmund Burke, Samuel Johnson and David Garrick among others. Others who attended included Lord Lyttleton, the Earl of Bath, Horace Walpole the Earl of Orford and Charles Burney.

On one level the gatherings could be seen as an 'informal intellectual meritocracy'; however, on another level they could be understood as an 'exclusive and hierarchically ordered hegemonic construct' (Pohl and Schellenberg, 2003: 2).

However, the influence of the individuals who formed the group gave it a specific character that gave the bluestockings, narrowly defined, both a conservative and exclusive profile. As the ideas of Montagu and others show, they established a moral and religious framework that equated the ideals of learning and virtue as part of an 'Anglican ideological project' that distinguished the bluestockings from more radical thinkers such as Mary Wollstonecraft and Catherine Macaulay. The bluestockings sought to frame their identity as 'moral and social models for the nation' (Pohl and Schellenberg, 2003: 2).

Bluestockings

The term 'bluestocking' is supposed to have emerged in quite an ad hoc fashion as outlined by one of the bluestockings, Frances Burney (1832: 262–3), who recalled:

> It owed its name to an apology made by Mr Stillingfleet, in declining to accept an invitation to a literary meeting of Mrs Vesey's, from not being, he said, in the habit of displaying a proper equipment for an evening assembly. 'Pho, pho,' cried she, with her well-known, yet always original simplicity, while she looked inquisitively at him and his accoutrements: '… don't mind dress. Come in your blue stockings!'

It was clear that the prestige of the bluestockings went far beyond the suburban and gentrified gatherings held in London, Bath and Dublin. Charles Burney wrote: 'My publication [*The Present State of Music in Germany, the Netherlands, and United Provinces*, 1773] was honoured with the approbation of the blue-stocking families at Mrs Vesey's and Mrs Montagu's and Sir Joshua Reynolds's, where I was constantly invited and regarded as a member.'

The exact membership of the bluestockings varied according to who was writing about them. Hannah More (1786), one of the most conservative women members of the group, in her famous poem *The Bas Bleu* or *Conversation*, outlines the following members of the bluestockings: Frances Boscawen, Elizabeth Montagu, Lord Lyttleton, William Pulteney, Horace Walpole, Elizabeth Carter and Elizabeth Vesey, as being among the main members of the circle. However, Walter S. Scott (1947) suggests a wider membership including: Mary Delany, Elizabeth Carter, Elizabeth Montagu, Hester Chapone, Hester Lynch Thrale, Hannah More, Frances Burney, Elizabeth Vesey, Frances Boscawen, Ann Ord, Catherine Talbot, Frances Greville, Anne Crewe, Charlotte Walsingham and Mary Monkton as hostess and members. More than just listing its members, More's poem provided a description of bluestocking practices and beliefs. It was published by Strawberry Hill Press, owned by Horace Walpole.

Beyond acting as an intellectual meeting point, the bluestockings emphasized an investment in education. Eger (2008: 32) points out that Montagu also used the term 'bluestocking college', which emphasized the sense in which the bluestocking circles invested in education at a time when women were denied access to university. Montagu was keen to establish links with the French salons on her trip to France in 1775, but Hannah More in *The Bas Bleu* sought to distance herself from the French salonnières.

Kelly (1999a: ix–xiv) points out that by the 1770s there was a change in the usage of the term bluestocking and it increasingly applied to only women in the group. And as Kelly states, it was used by those: 'who feared or felt excluded from Bluestocking Society'.

Elsewhere, Kelly (2001: 167, 169) shows that it is clear that politically, the first generation of bluestockings were committed to a 'progressive-aristocratic' programme that 'sought to amend traditional cultures of court libertinism and paternalism based on patronage and property essentially transforming them in terms of gentry and middle-class values'. Pohl and Schellenberg (2003: 6) also note that the early model was based on an 'essentialist and exclusive understanding of gender'. They argue that 'the "feminization" of culture that critics have found characteristic of the period was welcomed as positive, since women played the role of a civilizing force in the progression of commercial capitalism and political "embourgeoisement"'.

In fact Pohl and Schellenberg (2003: 6) show that separate gendered spheres were seen to be complementary in the 18th century, when modernizing and commercializing factors were developing. They make the interesting point that 'with conservative social critics opposed to the increasing commercialization of culture and blaming "effeminacy" and luxury for social ills, the nature of the feminine became a proxy in ideological disputes between conservatives and liberals'.

Thus the bluestockings occupied a contradictory position within the discourses of 18th-century femininity.

> While they furthered the advancement of women in education and in print publication, they at the same time enforced a feminine respectability that specifically concerned sexual conduct. For example, Catherine Macaulay's second marriage to the much younger and socially inferior William Graham in 1778 prompted defamatory attacks in bluestocking letters; Sarah Scott even went so far as to call upon the pure virgins and Virtuous Matrons who reside in this place [to] "unite and down her in the Avon" (Scott to Montagu, mo5391, 27 No[vember] 1778). Hester Lynch Thrale's 1784 second marriage to Gabriel Piozzi, an Italian musician and tutor of her daughter, was censured severely on the same grounds. (Pohl and Schellenberg, 2003: 7)

Nineteenth-century editors of bluestocking letters still felt the need to locate the bluestocking circle firmly within the domestic sphere and they put the emphasis on 'feminized realms' of Christian philanthropy and education (Pennington, 1817).

Kelly (2001: 177), in his article 'Bluestocking feminism', makes a significant political point in highlighting the differences between the gender politics of the bluestockings and the radical politics of the women intellectuals writing in the context of the political radicalism of the 1790s (see Chapter Three). The radical republicanism of Catherine Macaulay and the gender-equality rhetoric of Mary Wollstonecraft are in stark contrast to the conservative gender politics of the bluestockings. Kelly (2001: 177) describes the politics of the bluestockings as counter-Revolutionary politics and their domestic ideology as part of a 'remasculination of culture that characterised the Romantic movement'. While Kelly discusses the concept of 'bluestocking feminism', they were deeply conservative and followed the same pattern of other women writing in the 18th century in that they did not offer any attempt at reforming or transforming the condition or treatment of women.

However, the bluestockings and radicals did have some shared interests and concerns. As Eger (2008: 35) shows in 'The Bluestocking Legacy', both Wollstonecraft and Chapone had an interest in women's education and for a future generation of women. The bluestockings were able to establish through their own networks of patronage and bonds of friendship ways to offset the limitations that they experienced through culture and environment.

Despite the contradictory nature of the concept 'bluestocking feminism', Guest (2003: 60–1) argues that it can be seen to have a flexible definition:

> In its broadest sense, the term refers to women who were socially prominent not because they are aristocratic, and not always because they are wealthy, but because of their learning, because they are women of letters. More narrowly, the group can be taken to include most of the well-educated but not aristocratic women linked through correspondence as well as social interaction in London, Edinburgh, and perhaps Dublin, from around 1750 to the early decades of the nineteenth century.

Guest notes that the writings of the bluestockings were widely read in the second half of the 18th century. She cites Hester Chapone's *Letters on the Improvement of the Mind* (1773), which was written to her niece and became a standard text for young ladies, a handbook on the 'acquisition of middle-class femininity' (Guest, 2003: 60). In addition, Elizabeth Carter's work was seen as offering a significant contribution to scholarship and as an icon of national progress.

Elizabeth Montagu: mentoring and moralism

Elizabeth Montagu used her enormous wealth to establish a 'literary public' formed by the educated class but separate from the political public sphere. Her house in London's Portman Square, which she moved into in 1781, was a cross between a public building and a private house and she argued for a 'Bluestocking College' as serving an educative function for women who were denied access to university (see Eger, 2008: 32).

Guest (2005: 289) points out that Montagu 'was valued by her contemporaries for managing to transcend political factionalism, while nevertheless achieving political ends in that she removed men from their political context'. Montagu was responsible for developing the art of conversation as rational discourse, which was particularly important for women not only in terms of being leading participants in a mixed society of metropolitan culture but also as writers and educators.

Eger (2005: 290) notes that there were attempts from the end of the 17th century at establishing conversation between women and men in periodicals and contemporary literature; however, women were still generally restricted in what they were able to discuss. Despite this, members of the bluestocking circle both participated in and contributed to rational intellectual discourse. Eger (2005: 290–1) provides two examples of this.

> Elizabeth Montagu appealed to a patriotic pride in addressing directly Voltaire's criticism of Shakespeare in her widely acclaimed *Essays on the Writings and Genius of Shakespear with Some Remarks on the Misrepresentation of Msr Voltaire* which was published in 1769. In addition Elizabeth Carter was famous for having defined standard assumptions of 'female capacity' by making her living as a classical scholar. Her translation of Epictetus remained the standard English version until the beginning of the twentieth century.

Montagu was well established for her conversation, intercourse and undeniable cultural capital. But beyond this she was also well known for her patronage, which undoubtedly drew writers into the bluestocking circles. 'More significantly she propelled little known writers who might otherwise have not ventured forth into the literary public sphere. Bluestocking hostesses were pioneers in encouraging women from a diversity of backgrounds to participate in print culture' (Eger, 2005: 298).

Through her 'assemblies' or salons, which were associated with the idea of women supporting one another's literary endeavours, Montagu, among others, promoted women's education. In establishing such salons Montagu and the other bluestockings started to break down the boundaries between public and private spheres (see Chapter Two). As Eger (2005: 298) notes, 'her salon formed a semi-public arena in which women could freely exercise their opinions on most pressing topics of the day and form important connections with literary and political men in power'.

Montagu was also well established as a mentor. Her great wealth clearly facilitated her ability to act as a mentor to other women writers. Eger (2005: 298) states that she earned her income from coal mines in the North of England which allowed her to 'grant annuities to Elizabeth Carter, Hester Chapone, Sarah Fielding and her sister Sarah Scott. She also gave money to several charities on a regular basis. Hannah More described her as "the female Maecenas of Hill Street" (More, *Selected Writings*, 8–9)' (Eger, 2005: 298).

The bluestocking community, in its orientation and endeavours, was represented by Sarah Scott, the sister of Elizabeth Montagu, in her utopian novel *A Description of Millenium Hall*. The community as represented by Scott in her novel also advocated the bluestocking emphasis on 'rational self-improvement'. By 1800 and Montagu's death, the term bluestocking was synonymous with women writers and intellectuals.

Community of women as early public intellectuals

In addition to the contribution they made to women as 'public intellectuals' through their activities as 'theorists and practitioners of conversation', Eger (2005: 301) shows that the bluestockings also created a strong sense of community between women: 'By referencing the social habits of their peers, replacing cards and polite gossip with serious intellectual conversation, they were explicitly concerned to educate women, and implicitly to change contemporary attitudes with the relationship between idleness and work, leisure and scholarship.'

Guest (2003: 79–80) maintains that, while not directly involved in politics,

> Bluestocking forms of sociability in the 1760s and early 1770s could be understood as having an ambivalently political character precisely because of the ways in which their assemblies turned away from or smoothed over political differences. After the mid-1770s, that ambivalently political character becomes perhaps more distinctively associated with the gender of Bluestocking women than with their status as members of the educated classes; at the same time, male members became, because of their role in the 'world of letters', more clearly distinct from the unambiguous world of political participation.

Heller (1998) maintains that by the early 1780s, bluestockings were wistfully reflecting on an earlier time of relaxed sociability; but the political implications of this time of sociability or public life are not drawn out in her interesting essay. Guest shows that the educated class that helped the evolution of the literary sphere and who came together to form a 'bourgeois political public' at least created the 'fiction or fantasy of a feminine political voice' and created an opportunity for others such as 'Macaulay, Wollstonecraft and later Hays to think about gender as a collective identity in ways that were more directly and explicitly political' (Guest, 2003: 80).

Expansion of women public intellectuals

> The bluestocking community itself came to represent female scholarship in the public imagination. Its members cultivated this aspect of their identity by emphasising the reforming mission of the group to provide better education for women and to offer support for female authors. (Eger, 2005: 298)

Taylor (2005: 39) argues that historians of gender maintained that the 18th century was a time of hardening gender divisions, 'a period when men and women's lives bifurcated into separate spheres'. However, she claims that evidence provided by other historians, including Amanda Vickery, Margaret Hunt, Linda Colley and Olwen Hutton, shows that in fact the very opposite was happening by the second half of the 18th century and that 'the boundaries separating men and women were ... unstable and becoming more so' (Taylor, 2005: 41).

Taylor also counters what she claims is a tendency of historians of Enlightenment Britain to state that there is an absence of women from key sites of learning and debate, including academies, political associations, taverns and coffee-houses. Taylor (2005: 41) argues that against this 'must be set women's active presence in networks of enlightened sociability ... or the bluestocking salons of London and similar literary coteries in provincial centres of Enlightenment ... or the high-minded, politicised world of Rational Dissent where feminists of both sexes found ready support'.

Hesse (2005a: 259) has no doubt that women in large numbers took a leading part in the expansion of intellectual ideas in the 18th century in Europe. She shows 'that the number of women writers in France trebled to over 300 in print in the revolutionary decade alone'. She points out that the 'range of institutions within which women were both represented and in which they articulated their views included Masonic lodges, which were cosmopolitan in nature and could be found throughout Europe'. Hesse also identifies other mixed-sex intellectual settings, which she showed diverged along 'national, cultural and religious lines'. She also draws distinctions between France and England in terms of their relevance to the growth of public intellectuals. As Taylor (2005: 259) shows: 'In France, salons were spaces of hetero-social exchange from their inception in the early seventeenth century, whereas in England drawing room conversation was only designated in the latter half of the eighteenth century.'

Hesse also notes that there was an early and important distinction between Britain and Europe in terms of access to women intellectuals. In France and Italy, academies and learned societies offered honorific membership to women and allowed their attendance from the early years of the 18th century. However, she observes that Protestant countries were more reluctant to admit women. Hesse (2005a: 261) notes that 'almost all of these women of letters came from the upper ranks of European society: high court society, the landed gentry, the professions or the burgeoning ranks of royal officialdom throughout Europe'. She gives an interesting example of how much further advanced Europe was, as compared to Britain:

> Laura Bassi (1711–78), daughter of a lawyer, … in 1732 became the first woman to graduate from the University of Bologna, and the first woman to hold a university chair in any European university faculty. Her career marked not only the entry of women into the upper ranks of academia, but also the advent of a new model of feminine learning – the professional scientist rather than the clever dilettante. (Hesse, 2005a: 261)

Elsewhere, Heller (2015b: 3) argues that: 'The Bluestocking influence penetrated the full width and breadth of the cultural and political public ... because as opinion leaders, [they] functioned as a permeable membrane between smaller personal networks and the total network of society in which they were embedded.'

Pohl (2015), in an article entitled 'Cosmopolitan Bluestockings', looks at the bluestocking connection to France, Italy and Germany. Pohl maintains that some of the bluestockings such as Montagu had more extensive connections with the French salonnières and that all contributed to an international exchange of ideas, but that the idea of thinking about the bluestockings as cosmopolitan in an ideological sense is misplaced. Pohl (2015: 7) argues: 'For the bluestockings, any ideological commitment to a transnational, universal European culture was tempered by a self-centred and nationalistic patriotism that favoured an "exclusionary cosmopolitanism" ... because they modelled their universalistic ideals after the image of British culture and government.'

The role of the salon in the development of public intellectuals, particularly women public intellectuals, has been understated. Pohl (2015: 7) maintains that the salon as an institution played a special role in 'forging an egalitarian intellectual culture that cut across divisions of rank, gender and nation'.

Montagu was important in establishing early women public intellectuals. Kelly (2015: 186) maintains that she worked hard at establishing 'expected roles in the political, social and sexual-emotional economy of the social elites' and, as shown above, she became an important mentor for younger women writers. In addition, the marriage framework for many of the bluestocking women was unorthodox. Kelly shows that some in the circle created independent female-community households and argues that 'They supported each other's intellectual and cultural aspirations and attempts to achieve financial and social independence' (Kelly, 2015: 186).

As shown above, and as Kelly (2015: 187) indicates, Sarah Scott 'gave comprehensive literary expression to this gynocentric modernity in her novel *A Description of Millenium Hall* (1762) depicting a community of women, refugees from courtly upper-class exploitation of women, pursuing learning and the arts within a programme of social and economic philanthropic modernization on an estate previously ruined by extremes of upper-class extravagance and miserliness'.

Interestingly, Kelly also shows that correspondence between members of the bluestockings in the form of collections of letters – for example, from Montagu to Carter (Montagu, 1810), from Carter to Talbot and Vesey (Carter, 1809), and from Carter to Montagu (Montagu-Pennington, 1817) – were often edited by male family members and presented a much more domestic version of the literary lady.

Kelly, again moving the debate regarding women public intellectuals from the bluestockings into a wider context of understanding a broader field of women public intellectuals, identifies a range of other women, many of whom were not titled. He defines these women as serious and successful public intellectuals and included: Catherine Macaulay, Hester Thrale Piozzi, Elizabeth Lady Craven, later Margravine of Ansbach, Sydney Owenson, Lady Morgan, Eleanor Porden, Lady Franklin and

Byron's wife Anne Isabella, Baroness Byron. 'For them learning and work had somewhat different meanings, implications and uses than they had for Montagu's Bluestockings or their middle-class contemporaries' (Kelly, 2015: 193). Kelly notes that all could be defined as 'intellectuals' in the sense of the term at the time. He shows that they all contributed to a wide variety of specifically modern literature largely concerned with modernization for a range of professional and elite classes.

Backlash and the legacy

> Bookish women who flaunt their erudition are singled out for attack, as they were in most modernist writings on women. Animus against learned women particularly those displaying their wisdom in print, was a long-standing feature of British intellectual life that few Enlightenment writers sought to challenge. (Taylor, 2005: 39)

The legacy of the bluestockings can be seen to have taken several different forms. More positively, Scottish Enlightenment figures assigned them a central role in the rise of civil society and David Hume was particularly supportive. Eger shows how philosophers of the Scottish Enlightenment placed a new emphasis on the morally superior nature of women in accounts of the progress of man. However, Eger maintains that the lack of feminist recognition of the bluestockings' influence has to be set in the context of the backlash against the figure of the intellectual woman in the 19th century. Eger (2008: 126–7) notes that 'it was during this time that the term "bluestocking" acquired its most negative and misogynistic connotation'.

Eger (2008: 129) also notes that 'At the beginning of the nineteenth century, the combined social and intellectual prominence of so many intelligent women was greeted with suspicion and disgust by many men.' This was not just reflected in the work of male writers and philosophers but also by artists, such as in Rowlandson's *Breaking up of the Bluestocking Club*. Eger (2008: 127) shows that 'Rowlandson has chosen to emphasise the corporeality of his subjects rather than their mental accomplishments … it suggests a heady mixture of slovenliness, vanity and immorality (French cosmetics were widely associated with female narcissism)'.

Eger (2008: 132) also notes that another work, Daniel Maclise's (1836) lithograph *Regina's Maids of Honour*, 'domesticates intellectual women in order to make them more palatable, while at the same time belittling their achievements'. Eger shows that the most misogynistic and vitriolic attacks came from poets, writers and critics from the Romantic movement, including Samuel Taylor Coleridge, William Wordsworth and Lord Byron.

Conclusion

Thus, as has been shown, there was no single unitary conceptualization of what constituted 'bluestocking' philosophy. There were fault-lines within the thinking of the bluestockings along class, education and life-style. As Pohl and Schellenberg (2003: 3) show,

> rumours of opposing factions among the Bluestockings make it clear that these women's high profile attracted expressions of anxiety about learned and socially active women ... the Bluestockings as a specific cultural, social and political phenomenon played a crucial part in a widening and redefinition of women's social roles in the eighteenth century.

Regardless of these differences, the bluestockings established practices and a philosophy that acted to bridge public and private spheres in the 18th century. As Eger (2005: 300) comments,

> From being viewed as mediating and socialising figures, the bluestockings came to be considered and represented as a literary community in the public sphere. Their reforming attitude to literature and sociability should be understood in the context of pleas for better education for women. Later and more radical writers, such as Anna Barbauld and Mary Wollstonecraft were arguably inspired by the bluestocking model, seeking out the conversation of men as equals.

Chapter Two focuses more specifically on the significance of the public and private sphere as areas that theorists such as Habermas provided with theoretical insights.

TWO

Gender and the politics of the public sphere

Introduction

The bluestockings established a set of literary, civic and political discourses that provided a framework for the opening up of literary and political movements, including the Bloomsbury Group and the suffrage movement. Habermas's (1989: 55–6) understanding of the 'bourgeois public sphere' is central in this respect. He distinguished between two forms of 'public'. Firstly, 'the world of letters', where Habermas described 'privatized individuals in their capacity as human beings [who] communicated through critical debate and secondly the "political realm"', which Habermas described as 'private people in their capacity as owners of commodities [who] communicated through rational-critical debate'. Guest (2003: 65), drawing on Hannah More, notes that by the late 18th century there was a social world of the educated elite. She notes that this could go beyond the bluestockings and 'constituted something resembling Habermas's notion of the literary public formed by the educated class'.

Guest (2003: 78) shows that the bluestockings' distance from politics epitomizes the gendered character of the public sphere in the 18th century: 'the feminine right to Habermas's public world of letters seems to be confirmed by its juxtaposition with the political realm'. Guest skilfully draws on Habermas's relationship of the educated classes with the bourgeois political public sphere to understand the way in which bluestocking society established the potential of a feminine political voice. As Guest (2003: 80) shows, it: 'may have made it possible for more explicitly political writers such as Macaulay, Wollstonecraft and later Hays to think about gender as a collective identity in ways that were more directly and explicitly political.'

Pohl and Schellenberg (2003: 11), in their analysis of Habermas's contribution to an understanding of 18th-century writings, state that

Habermas offers an account of the emergence of the bourgeois public sphere in the eighteenth century, relating its genesis to profound social and economic changes that transformed early modern Europe from absolutism to mercantilism to a modern civil society. Feminist studies of the eighteenth century have noted that Habermas's interpretation elides questions of the gendered specificity of the public and private.

A variety of feminist scholars (Landes, 2013; Meehan, 2013; Wilson, 1995, among others) are critical of Habermas's model as hegemonic, exclusive and gendered. Others see more scope in Habermas's model, Guest (2003) 'suggests that the discourse of the private and domestic allows women to intervene in public and political affairs if it linked to a specifically conservative notion of propriety and patriotism'. Guest argues further that domesticity can be '"a site from which an oppositional political discourse can be articulated"' (cited in Pohl and Schellenberg, 2003: 12). By contrast, Moore (1997) sees the reliance on the 'domestic' as complicit in the formation of gendered discourses of power. She uses Sarah Scott's novel *A Description of Millenium Hall* as an example of this. 'More argues that while public/private ideologies might empower women within the domestic realm, they also legitimize bourgeois hierarchies and power relations' (Pohl and Schellenberg, 2003: 12).

Pohl and Schellenberg see literary salons such as those established by the bluestockings as bridging the public and private divide. As they note: 'Literary salons may have been located in the intimate domestic sphere, the salon, the parlor, or the *ruelle*, but were nothing less than an expansion of the authentic public sphere into institutions of "intellectual sociability"' (2003: 12). These splits in the approach to the public/private framing of the debates were matched by splits in the types of women intellectuals, with the bluestockings viewing other women intellectuals, including Susannah Wesley, Lady Huntington and Catherine Macaulay, with suspicion. For these women intellectuals, the emphasis was on the public/political rather than the private.

Lanser (2003) argues that the concept of 'Bluestocking Circle' is seen as having a more generic conceptualization that encompasses 'a coalition of femininity, philanthropy, Anglican piety, English propriety, and intellectual pursuit all integrated into a public identity that could promote women's participation in literary culture as "decorous, salutary and safe"' (Pohl and Schellenberg, 2003: 18).

Habermas, the public world of letters and the political realm

Habermas's distinction between two forms of the public provides for Guest (2003) a useful framework for comprehending his contribution to understanding the emergence of women public intellectuals. As stated earlier, Guest (2003: 62–3) notes that he distinguishes between two forms of the public: '"the world of letters", where "privatized individuals in their capacity as human beings communicated through critical debate", and the "political realm", where "private people in their capacity as owners of commodities communicated through rational–critical debate"'.

Guest (2003: 63) goes on to show that for Habermas the two spheres, the 'world of letters' and 'the political realm' were distinct: 'the circle of people who made up the two forms of public were not ... completely congruent'. Habermas argues that women and dependents were excluded from the political public sphere (factually and legally). However, he argues that they took a more active part in the literary public sphere than did those who owned private property. Habermas identifies those who took part in 'the literary public sphere' as 'female readers as well as apprentices and servants' (cited in Guest, 2003: 63).

Regardless of this incongruity, Habermas maintains that 'the fully developed bourgeois public sphere was based on the fictitious identity of the two roles assumed by the privatised individuals who come together to form a public: the role of property owners and the role of human beings pure and simple'. Guest (2003: 63) shows that Habermas attributed to the 'educated classes', who are responsible for the 'self-understanding of public opinion', this fiction of the identity of property owners who have a political voice, and human beings who are merely literary subjects'.

Thus Guest (2003: 78) notes: 'The feminine right to Habermas's public world of letters seems to be confirmed by its juxtaposition with the political real', which, as shown was an entirely masculinist domain of 'rational–critical debate'. She also shows that after the mid-1770s the ambivalently political character of educated women in literary circles becomes perhaps more directly associated with the gender of bluestocking women than with their status as members of the educated classes. Female members of an educated public intellectual elite, because of their role the 'world of letters', become more clearly distinct from the unambiguously masculine world of political participation.

As Guest (2003: 80) shows, despite this, 'Bluestocking sociability may thus have made available the fiction or fantasy of a feminine political voice – or at least may have made it possible for more explicitly political writers such Macaulay, Wollstonecraft, and later Hays to think about gender as a collective identity in ways that were more directly and explicitly political.'

Gender, feminism and the public and private spheres

Implicit in the debate on the public and private spheres is a debate about rights and citizenship and, as Pateman (1989: 118) points out, it is ultimately what the feminist movement is about. Pateman is an important counter to the views of Habermas and she points out the dangers of ignoring sexual difference in attempting to understand political difference. She makes the following point: 'Political theorists argue about the individual, and take it for granted that their subject matter concerns the public world, without investigating the way in which the "individual", "civil society" and the "public" have been constituted as patriarchal categories in opposition to womanly nature and the "private sphere"' (Pateman, 1988: 29).

The American Declaration of Independence and the French Declaration of the Rights of Man put forward new definitions of human equality, rights and political freedom that did not fully address women's rights. While more radical writers such as Macaulay and Wollstonecraft (see Chapter Three) argued for a broader definition of rights for the female population they did not countenance the idea of women's rights. Wollstonecraft argued that full citizenship should be extended to all, but was ambivalent about the position of working-class women (see Chapter Three).

Habermas: the public sphere as an intermediary space

The public sphere was for Habermas a forum where members of the public could meet and rationally debate affairs of state. He sees it as an intermediary space, between the intimate sphere of the family and the politics of the state. It is defined as a 'space free from prejudice and separate from the government, in which authority was held up to public scrutiny and the "common good" of the people was debated' (Eger, 2001: 7). Eger shows that in his model Habermas is entirely ambivalent about the position of women in the public sphere:

> Habermas places great emphasis on a number of new mainly urban institutions such as the salons, coffeehouses

and taverns that flourished in eighteenth century society. While he acknowledges the presence of women in the public sphere as readers, his attitude to them is always ambiguous. At times he appears to welcome the gradual exclusion of women as a necessary prelude to the process whereby debates within the republic of letters assumed an increasingly political function.

Habermas's view of the emergence of the public sphere is a gendered one. Not only did he position women outside the sphere of public space but he did not see women as making a significant contribution to opinions generated within the public sphere. Eger (2001: 8) outlines the historical and conceptual inaccuracies in his thinking:

> The inaccuracy of Habermas's assumption that only men were admitted to the coffee-house is compounded by his assumption that female opinion was inconsequential whereas male opinion was of value to the public sphere. His allusion to salon culture is a necessary reminder that he adhered to a historical narrative in which the dominance of aristocratic models (and their implied accessibility to women) gave way to a society characterised by men of the professional and commercial middle-classes. In developing his account, Habermas emphasises the role of male property owners in the formation of the public sphere, omitting women altogether from its developments as he does in his description of an idealised realm of print culture with clear political functions.

Many feminists have taken issue with Habermas's perspective on gender. Gonda (2001) emphasises how women were highly visible in the public sphere as it focused on issues of respectability and an exposure of their private lives, as is the case with Macaulay and Wollstonecraft. Eger also shows that women were not just objects but also subjects in the public sphere. She cites the example of Eliza Haywood, who was editor of the journal *The Female Spectator* (see Chapter Four), which established opinions on a wide range of subjects of a cultural, political and religious nature. As Eger writes (2001: 10), 'Haywood's concern to "hit the reigning humour" by providing gossip and current affairs without sacrificing the moral benefits of individual instruction shows a shrewd awareness of the potential pitfalls of public opinion.'

The extent of women's involvement in the public sphere went well beyond Haywood's work, influential though it was. Eger shows that a number of women, including Mary Wollstonecraft, Hannah More, Charlotte Smith, Elizabeth Carter and Elizabeth Inchbald, were reliant on their literary earnings but also conveyed significant ideas about gender and society in their writings. Catherine Macaulay (see Chapter Three) was prolific in the historical and political publishing that she engaged in. Eger (2001: 14) shows that Macaulay's political pamphlet *A Modest Plea for the Protection of Copyright* (1774) 'makes explicit links between the professionalization of writing and the emergence of a middle class increasingly determined to assert independence'.

What Habermas's work does is point to a change in the class nature of the intelligentsia since the emergence of the bluestockings, which was a hugely significant aspect of the public sphere and growth of public intellectuals. The aristocratic and wealthy nature of the bluestockings was expanded into a much more broadly based conceptualization of 'the professional'. Eger (2001: 14) shows how this worked in practice:

> women were active in the trades related to a rising professional literary (and literate) class: Anna Yearsley, 'the milk-woman poet', set up a circulating library; Susannah Duncombe, daughter of the artist Joseph Highmore and a close friend of Elizabeth Carter and Hester Chapone, was an engraver and book illustrator; others were involved in the book trade as printers and publishers.

More generally, women were very involved in an expanding education and print culture and in extending literacy, which fundamentally supported the expansion of a public intelligentsia.

Eger (2001: 15) claims that whereas feminists have defined the Enlightenment as a monolithic, patriarchal movement she and others have shown that it is clear that women as well as men were influential in defining the terms of the intellectual expansion that is defined as the Enlightenment. In fact this period can be seen as a watershed in terms of shifting the definition of '"learned ladies" from bluestockings to cosmopolitan intellectuals'.

Kelly (2001) sees the bluestockings as 'remodelling' intellectual culture so that women could achieve greater participation. He sees this as coinciding with a movement towards the advancement of 'moral virtue' and 'gentry capitalism'. Kelly shows that this experimentation with new forms of 'intellectual exchange' and 'self-fashioning' led to a greater experimentation with different literary forms.

Other feminist thinkers (Landes, 2013; Meehan, 2013) have shown how Habermas neglected other areas of significance for understanding gender and the public sphere. Landes (2013) shows the limitations of Habermas's position:

> she argues his estimation of the liberatory potential of the public sphere is too sanguine and his description of its emancipatory mechanisms too narrow. Describing the public sphere as one in which private people come together as a public in and through the use of reason, Habermas locates its obstacles in the slippage between the actual and the ideal, and not in the notion of the public sphere itself … The exclusion of the private sphere of emotions and of the personal relations in which they are initiated and sustained constituted the de facto institutions of the press and literature … The Habermasian public sphere identified with equality and reason, favors certain abilities and interests over others and in effect … excludes the problematisation of the gender-determined power differential in the intimate sphere, insuring that male subjects would be its dominant inhabitants. (Meehan, 2013: 8–9)

Fleming (2013), in 'Women and the "Public Use of Reason"', assesses Habermas's account of the structure of the private and the political, focusing on Habermas's account of the emergence of the public, private and intimate spheres. She argues that Habermas is wrong to see the exclusion of women from the bourgeois public sphere as simply the failure of the bourgeoisie to realize its own normative ideals. She argues that the exclusion was actually constitutive of the institutionalization of the sphere.

In fact, Fleming maintains that Habermas sees structural changes around gender relations as part of the development of the bourgeois public sphere. Fleming encourages us to consider the way that intimacy is structured in gender terms, which she argues shows the extent to which the 'personal is political' and the 'political is personal'. Fleming believes that, despite limitations in Habermas's work, feminists can use his distinctions between the public, private and intimate spheres to further their analysis to illuminate and theorize a range of issues in making distinctions between the public and the private.

Landes (2013: 96) shows how class and its associated characteristics – property, income, literacy and cultural background – were key elements leading to access to the bourgeois public sphere. Landes does cite one area that Habermas identifies that was more broadly based and attracted people from across the social categories. This was the English coffee-house where 'the poor artisan craftsman, and shopkeeper mingled with their betters' (Habermas, 1989: 32–3). However, they were not open to women. In gender terms, the bourgeois public sphere was a restricted male preserve, with the exception of salon society that was shaped by women. Habermas suggests that the exclusion of women from the English coffee-houses could have been an advantage in so far as 'critical debate ignited by works of literature and art was soon extended to include economic and political disputes without any guarantee … that such discussion would be inconsequential, at least in the immediate context' (Habermas, 1989: 32–3).

Fraser (1990) maintains that from a variety of historical research into the public sphere, Habermas failed to examine examples of non-liberal, non-bourgeois or competing public spheres, and that as a result 'he ends up idealizing the liberal public sphere'. She comments that 'in both stratified and egalitarian societies, a multiplicity of publics is preferable to a single public sphere; and that an adequate conception of the public sphere would countenance the inclusion, not exclusion of interest and issues "that bourgeois masculinist ideology labels 'private' and treats as inadmissible"' (Fraser, 1990: 61).

Gender, rights and the public and private spheres

> In the type of liberal context that aspires to justice and equal opportunity for all, there are two tasks for the political cultivation of emotion. One is to engender and sustain strong commitment to worthy projects that require effort and sacrifice – such as social redistribution, the full inclusion of previously excluded or marginalized groups, the protection of the environment, foreign aid, and the national defense. (Nussbaum, 2013: 3)

Nussbaum (2013), and as shown in a number of analyses (Philips, 2001; Mackenzie, 2009), raises the issue of the relationship between feminism and liberalism and focuses on the issue of the intersection of rights with emotions. In some ways, and as noted by Philips (2001: 250), Nussbaum, in *Sex and Social Justice* (1999), provides a critique of Judith Butler, who views all normative positions as inherently dictatorial. As Philips (2001: 250) shows: 'Nussbaum counters this with a theory of human justice that is liberal humanist, and feminist. In doing so, she tackles head on the supposed conflict between liberalism and feminism, arguing that "liberal individualism, consistently carried through entails a radical feminist program".'

Nussbaum shares with Pateman (1988, 1989) a critique of liberal contractualism, where Pateman makes two charges: 'The first is that liberalism for men was based on subordination for women, so that the social contract concluded between separate and autonomous men was premised on a prior sexual contract that delivered the control of women' (Philips, 2001: 253). Pateman also argues that liberalism generated an understanding of individuals as the owners of their own bodies and capacities, not therefore beholden to anyone else for the disposition of these, but entitled to enter into contracts with other individuals for the use of their talents and capacities. Pateman regards this as inherently unsatisfactory. Pateman's point is that liberalism has drawn on notions of self-ownership for its understanding of freedom and choice, and that in doing so it reflects a misleading masculine model of human interaction.

Underpinning Nussbaum's argument is the reason/emotion dichotomy, and this was central in understanding a range of conceptualizations in the forefront of rights issues, including dichotomies between mind/body, reason/emotion, justice/care, which were seen to characterize debates between men and women. A central feature of all Nussbaum's work is that she sees liberalism as too tied to rationalistic thinking: 'that by placing all emphasis on reason as a mark of humanity it has emphasised a trait that all males traditionally prize, and denigrated traits such as emotion and imagination, that females traditionally prize' (Nussbaum, 1999: 74).

Emerging women public intellectuals in the public sphere

Kelly (2015) shows that there was an expanded membership of the bluestockings and a more extended agenda. Kelly mentions a number of other women, including Mary Delany (1700–88), Christian Isobel Johnstone (1781–1857), mathematician Mary Somerville (1780–1872) and feminist writer and philosopher Harriet Martineau (1806–76) (see Brooks, 2014). Kelly identifies a different and wider group, including those from the 'belles lettres and fine arts'. They were captured in part in Richard Samuel's The Nine Living Muses of Great Britain, which was exhibited in the Royal Academy in 1779.

A further indicator of the expanding role of women as public intellectuals was the 1788 Catalogue of Five Hundred Celebrated Authors of Great Britain Now Living. Kelly (2015: 182–3) shows that this included 31 women, among them 'literary ladies' (Macaulay, Graham, Montagu,

Lennox, Piozzi, Reeve and Williams). Some enjoyed critical respect and even celebrity (Frances Burney, Ann Francis, Charlotte Smith, Anna Seward, Harriet and Sophie Lee, Elizabeth Inchbald, Sarah Trimmer, Hannah Cowley and Lady Eglantine Wallace), some were controversial.

Interestingly, Kelly (2015: 183) comments that the term 'intellectual' in today's sense of the word and its meaning as 'devoted to academic and cultural interests' was only emerging as a concept at the time, and from the newspapers and magazines of the time, it rarely applied to women until the 1820s and 1830s.

Conclusion

The Habermasian distinction between the 'public world of letters' and the 'political realm' provides a useful distinction in terms of gender and the politics of the public sphere. It certainly provides a framework for situating the bluestockings within the bourgeois public sphere. However, as has been shown in this chapter a range of feminist writers and theorists have highlighted the limitations of the concept of the public sphere as put forward by Habermas, and the conception of the liberal bourgeois public sphere has significant limitations. The distinction between public and private spheres is also about rights and the writings of public intellectuals. Catherine Macaulay and Mary Wollstonecraft recognize the implications for democracy and republicanism. Within the Habermasian model the concept of the intelligentsia and the public intellectual moved from the aristocracy to a more broadly based conception of the professional. This chapter has also reflected on contemporary feminist theorists' conceptualization of rights and politics, including Martha Nussbaum, Carol Pateman and Anne Philips.

THREE

'Uncompromising politics': Mary Wollstonecraft and Catherine Macaulay

> You are the only female writer who I coincide with respecting the rank our sex ought to endeavour to attain in the world. I respect Mrs Macaulay Graham because she contends for laurels whilst most of her sex only seek for flowers. (Letter from Mary Wollstonecraft to Catherine Macaulay, 30 December, 1790, cited in Hill, 1995: 177)

Introduction

Catherine Macaulay and Mary Wollstonecraft are considered to be the two most important women writers on politics and society in late 18th-century England. Macaulay (1763–83) had achieved international fame and kudos with her eight-volume *History of England from the Accession of James 1 to that of the Brunswick Line*, which was a generation before the publication of Wollstonecraft's (1792) *A Vindication of the Rights of Woman*. Gunther-Canada (2003: 49), in her analysis of Catherine Macaulay and Mary Wollstonecraft, shows that they advocate distinct notions of gender politics. As she comments: 'Their texts are powerful examples of women's participation in eighteenth century debates about civic education that reveal how class privilege, gender ideology, and religious beliefs could complicate and compromise arguments for women's political rights.' She goes on to show that 'Catherine Macaulay and Mary Wollstonecraft offer different models of voice and advocacy for women in the historical discourse on civic virtue' (Gunther-Canada, 2003: 49).

Peltz (2008: 95), in 'A Revolution in Female Manners', maintains that from the American Declaration of Independence in 1776 to the end of the Napoleonic Wars in 1815, Britain's economic, social and political stability was in turmoil. She argues that 'against the background of revolution in America and France, relations between the sexes – and the proper roles of each – were increasingly challenged'.

Peltz maintains that the turmoil surrounding this time can be seen 'in the reception and troubled reputation of a new generation of political voices: the republican Catherine Macaulay, the radical Mary Wollstonecraft and the conservative Hannah More'.

Hill (1992: 130) describes Macaulay (but it equally applies to Wollstonecraft) as: 'a woman in a man's world, unorthodox and [an] anti-establishment figure'. Both writers were important in the development of political thought, and Wollstonecraft was particularly important in the development of early feminist thought. As shown earlier, Guest (2003: 61) maintains that by the 1790s 'Catherine Macaulay and Mary Wollstonecraft had achieved a kind of political articulacy and a degree of public audibility that are central to the emergence of modern feminist politics in Britain'. In addition, both Macaulay and Wollstonecraft were shown as woman public intellectuals who could defend republican political principles.

Both contributed to debates on education, and Macaulay believed in the same education for women and men. However, Macaulay was less concerned with the position of women in society than Wollstonecraft was. While they were both interested in democracy and equal rights for women and men, Macaulay was in favour of full male suffrage but did not raise the question of women's suffrage. Neither writer was supportive of full suffrage for women, and both believed that working-class women did not have the necessary capacity and responsibility for suffrage.

Both shared with many in the 'Bluestocking Circle' reservations about 'lower class women', assuming political rights as being in practice restricted to women of the 'propertied classes' (Hill 1995: 185). This view of women's rights was not untypical of how they were understood by 18th-century radicals.

In some of their most important works, Wollstonecraft's (1792) *A Vindication of the Rights of Woman* and Macaulay's (1790a) *Letters on Education*, they are critical of educating women to make them 'more attractive for men', but Wollstonecraft goes further than Macaulay in arguing that the education of women should be about giving them more independence. In addition, Wollstonecraft maintained that women should work and become independent (as she herself had done). Porter (2004) sees Wollstonecraft's feminism as being in a general trend towards sexual liberation and acknowledges Wollstonecraft and Godwin as 'the Enlightenment's premier husband and wife team'.

Public and private spheres in the work of Wollstonecraft and Macaulay

Wiseman (2001: 16) shows how Macaulay bridged public and private spheres. She argues that Macaulay's career indicates the dynamic relationship between public and private, 'inviting us to complicate Habermas's sense of the public sphere' as demarcated by critical reason used by 'private people' whose participation was guaranteed by propertied citizenship. Wiseman charts the shift from respect to denigration in public responses to Macaulay's life and work. Jacobus (2001: 275) shows how Wollstonecraft's private life and the critique generated by Godwin's memoirs reveal moving boundaries between private and public. 'Godwin's memoir goes further, not only revealing that Wollstonecraft and Godwin "did not marry" until after her second pregnancy, but that Wollstonecraft had not married her previous lover, the American democrat, Gilbert Imlay (the father of her first child, Fanny).'

Jacobus (2001: 275) goes on to say that Godwin's memoir 'allowed the anti-Jacobins to represent Wollstonecraft as a "public" woman with "French" morals and to discredit her programme for reforming relations between the sexes (especially marriage) as libertinage'. As Jacobus shows, Godwin's 'memoirs of Wollstonecraft set out to redraw the always fluctuating boundaries between the personal and the public, bringing both intimacy and indiscretion into the realm of political debate'.

'Revolutionary feminism': the philosophy of Mary Wollstonecraft

In his book *Revolutionary Feminism: The Mind and Career of Mary Wollstonecraft*, Kelly (1992) argues that Wollstonecraft represented an important shift in the relationship between learning and work, class and gender 'in a modernization led by and for the same professional and commercial middle ranks to which she, Barbauld, and similar women of modern learning belonged'.

Kelly (2015: 195) shows how Wollstonecraft identified herself as an early public intellectual, 'as the "first of a new genus", what she called "a female philosopher", a woman who supported herself by literary – intellectual work that also critiqued forms of unmodernity and promoted a certain version of modernization'.

Kelly also notes that, just as her predecessors Macaulay and Barbauld had done, Wollstonecraft challenged and experimented with conventional male-dominated discourse such as historiography and philosophy, 'hybridized them, and popularised them as the appropriate work of the specifically female "philosopher" or public intellectual'. In doing so, as Kelly notes, she wanted to demonstrate the capacity of women to modernize themselves and to perform literary intellectual work and thereby become an 'exemplar of (a particular version of) modernization' (Kelly, 2015: 195).

As is shown in Chapter Four, Wollstonecraft's *Maria or the Wrongs of Woman* (1798) and *Mary: A Fiction* (1788) are more directly political in their response to the revolution of the 1790s and social class, and also challenge conventions around female behaviour as well as a critique of those criticizing the French Revolution.

The gender politics of Mary Wollstonecraft

Wollstonecraft is seen as adding different dimensions into political theory to incorporate personal relations and emotional experience. Sapiro (1992: xiv) maintains that in doing so she brings into consideration the 'conditions of ordinary citizens'. Caine (1997: 24) makes the important point the focus on the political dimensions of personal and emotional relations is central in Wollstonecraft's work – and indeed to that of modern feminism – and argues that it makes Wollstonecraft's *Vindication* what she describes as 'a founding text' of Anglo-American feminism. As Caine comments, the key element is that the social and political turmoil of the 1790s provided a framework in which the connection between women and the political world could be made.

In her books *A Vindication of the Rights of Men* and *A Vindication of the Rights of Woman*, Wollstonecraft developed her strongest ideas on gender relations and also established women's oppression as a political issue. Caine (1997: 26) also shows that Wollstonecraft took issue with Burke's sexual stereotyping and depiction of women. In *The Rights of Men* she singled out the sexual attitudes behind some of his commentary, and in *The Rights of Woman* she made a specific response to legislation that established a new system of education for boys but not for girls. Caine maintains that Wollstonecraft was outraged by 'the gendering of moral qualities' and saw it as central in the discussion of women. Wollstonecraft challenged the existence of 'sexed virtues' and demanded instead 'a single set of human virtues with the same meaning for men and women' (Wollstonecraft, 1792a: 91, cited in Caine, 1997: 27). Caine maintains that Wollstonecraft argued for a rational approach to education and employment so that women had economic independence from marriage. Wollstonecraft specifically cites the study of medicine and business as proper professional pursuits, while also recommending the study of politics and history as intellectual pursuits.

Despite a commitment to rights for women and men, Wollstonecraft did not go so far as to recommend the enfranchisement of women in *A Vindication of the Rights of Woman*. However, while not demanding the vote, she connected every discussion of women's education, of motherhood and of women's work with independence and citizenship (Wollstonecraft, 1792a: 223). Caine (1997: 28) makes the point that while Wollstonecraft's work was the subject of significant criticism because it neglected the issue of the enfranchisement of women, in the 1920s when women were given the vote, Wollstonecraft's book was seen as an important text because of its concern with questions about sexual double standards.

The issue of heterosexual love is dealt with in Wollstonecraft's novel *Maria, or the Wrongs of Woman* (1798), which is regarded as her most significant feminist work as it addresses issues of marriage and sexuality for both working-class and middle-class women, as well as friendship between women. Caine (1997: 38) states that *Vindication* shows Wollstonecraft's emancipatory potential for women, whereas *Maria* shows her disillusionment with the French Revolution in relation to democracy and women.

Women's rights in the work of Mary Wollstonecraft

Stetson-McBridge (1996: 168) states that, in writing two books on the question of rights, one on women's rights and one on men's rights, Wollstonecraft argued that rights belong to both. Wollstonecraft argues that the basis for differentiation between women and men should not be sex but variations in the qualities of reason and virtue. She argues that since women and men have equal capacities for reason there is no natural superiority of men.

Stetson-McBridge also clarifies why Wollstonecraft uses the word 'woman' rather than 'women'. She argues that discussion of gender issues in the 18th and 19th centuries often used the term woman, and she maintains that this was heavily influenced by the translation of documents written in French. While Wollstonecraft argued that women are equal to men as human beings and citizens, she also insisted that women's special place in the political community should be recognized, and she argued that women need not take the same roles as men in order to have rights. As Wollstonecraft (1792b [1988]:

145) states: 'The being who discharges the duties of its station is independent; and speaking of women at large, the first duty is to themselves as rational creatures, and the next, in point of importance, as citizens, is that, which includes so many, of a mother.'

Stetson-McBridge sees Wollstonecraft's political theory in the liberal tradition that Pateman (1988) maintains is integral to the public/private divide. She further argues that Wollstonecraft integrates her focus on government and public matters with private and familial concerns (Stetson-McBridge, 1996: 171). In addition, and in order to develop the capacity for reason, independence and citizenship, Wollstonecraft (1792 [1988]: 157–8) advocates a system of national education for boys and girls. She comments as follows:

> to render also the social compact truly equitable, and in order to spread those enlightening principles, which alone can ameliorate the fate of man, women must be allowed to found their virtue on knowledge, which is scarcely possible unless they be equated by the same pursuits as men. (Wollstonecraft, 1792 [1988]: 173)

The other factor for Wollstonecraft is the need for women to become independent by earning their own subsistence, as she notes:

> Nor will women ever fulfil their peculiar duties of their sex, till they become enlightened citizens, till they become free by being able to earn their own subsistence, independent of men, in the same manner ... Nay marriage will never be sacred till women by being brought up with men are prepared to be their companions rather than their mistresses. (Wollstonecraft, 1792 [1988]: 165)

In a related article on the relationship between women's rights and the US Supreme Court, Miller (1996) draws the implications of Wollstonecraft's attempt to transpose the 'inalienable rights of men' from the American and French Revolutions to include women. Wollstonecraft believed that if they could be given equal opportunities such as educational advantages, they could attain to all the same achievements as men. Miller (1996: 153) notes that in the US women had more educational opportunities towards the end of the 19th century, and that by that time, 3,000 female students were enrolled in institutions of higher education that offered a standard academic curriculum.

Miller also maintains that the US Supreme Court was slow to grant women constitutional equality in any sphere. She further observes:

> States could decide whether or not it was appropriate for women to vote while the Court accepted and reinforced the state's views that a woman's destiny lay not in the public sphere but in the domestic realm (it was not until 1920 that this decision was abrogated by the passage of the Nineteenth Amendment to the U.S. Constitution which gave women the right to vote). (Miller, 1996: 154)

Miller makes an interesting commentary on the Supreme Court's approach to gender rights. As she comments:

> Until well into the twentieth century, Supreme Court jurisprudence was consistent with the previous century's rulings on gender-rights issues. The Court's position was that women were born differently from men and this could be treated constitutionally different, even if it worked to women's detriment ... For example in 1908 the Court interpreted the Fourteenth Amendment somewhat differently than before and found it provided substantive support for ameliorating the harsh working conditions of women in certain establishments. (Miller, 1996: 154–5)

However, Miller (1996: 155) notes that the Court's rationale was not based on notions of equality of opportunity, but on paternalistic views of the proper role of women in society. Miller shows how the Court has been criticized for its decisions contrary to the reproductive freedom rights of women. This includes allowing states to prohibit public employees and public facilities from assisting with and performing abortions.

Wollstonecraft, political theory and political discourse

Wollstonecraft challenged the tradition of political rights and political writing and rewrote the political discourse to include women. In *A Vindication of the Rights of Men* (1790) she replies to Edmund Burke's attack on the humanist ideals of the French Revolution and 'underscored the profound exclusion of women from both the discourse and practice of Enlightenment philosophy' (Gunther-Canada, 1996: 61).

There is little doubt that Wollstonecraft's *Vindications* were radical publications on the discourse of rights in the 18th century and have implications for feminist theory because they highlight the problematic nature of political discourse that excludes women's rights. As noted previously, the essence of the problem was the traditional position held by late 18th-century philosophers, which was the distinction between women's nature and rationality. In fact Gunther-Canada (1996: 77 n5) maintains that Ralph Wardle, Wollstonecraft's biographer, repeatedly argued that the limitations of *Rights of Men* arose from 'Wollstonecraft's unsuitability as a woman for writing political theory'. Wardle criticizes Wollstonecraft for 'abusing Burke'.

However, Gunther-Canada (1996: 77 n5) shows that Wollstonecraft's 'innovative attempt to use the philosophical fathers to dispute patriarchal politics ... displays her intellectual engagement with political theory'. She goes on to say that, in doing so, Wollstonecraft challenges the masculine in language politics. But Wollstonecraft goes further than simply challenging the discursive terrain, as Gunther-Canada (1996: 62) comments: 'She takes on the "gothic pile" of hereditary property and honor which were handed from father and son amid the heraldry of patriarchy and primogeniture.'

Thus Wollstonecraft, as well as providing a feminist critique of the association of reason with authority, went further: 'Wollstonecraft's appropriation of the manly authority of Enlightenment reason added to her analysis of the tensions between property and equality, provided an immanent critique of the sexual politics of the late eighteenth century political theory' (Gunther-Canada, 1996: 62). Gunther-Canada shows the feminist emphasis of Wollstonecraft's thinking: '*The Rights of Woman* links the textual representation of women as sexual beings devoid of reason to the silence of women in the discourses that shape their lives. Wollstonecraft thus skilfully unites philosophical argument with discursive strategy to articulate a theory of women's rights.'

Wollstonecraft's *Rights of Woman* achieves a dual objective in challenging the 'humanist discourse on rights' through analysing how femininity is constructed in the work of male philosophers, 'who claim to derive their portrait of woman from nature' (Gunther-Canada, 1996: 63). Written in the late 18th century, Wollstonecraft's language is fiercely combative of male writings and practice and 'attacks the "boasted prerogative of man,"... which subjects women to the tyranny of male prejudice in their own homes and in the Houses of Parliament' (1989: 170). Wollstonecraft calls for a 'revolution in female manners', which she maintains will provide women with the educational, economic and political means to allow them to revolutionize their identities.

Interestingly, Gunther-Canada shows how Wollstonecraft's feminism reflects some of the issues around subjectivity that are resonant of contemporary feminist debates. As she comments: 'Wollstonecraft's own attempt to create a universal subject who transcends class and gender, is itself confounded by her recognition that Enlightenment philosophy reflects a reified model of subjectivity' (Gunther-Canada, 1996: 64). Despite the feminism of Wollstonecraft's discourse, Gunther-Canada notes that it is telling that she refuses to identify herself as a woman in the text where she refutes Burke's representation of women as 'passive, private, and most important silent' (1996: 64).

Wollstonecraft's two *Vindications* opened up debates about the normative structures that limited women's access to political participation. As Gunther-Canada (1996: 69–70) comments: 'Her *Vindication of the Rights of Men* represents a first and necessary step in the development of a political theory that could encompass new and diverse models of female citizenship.' She further notes that 'Wollstonecraft's second *Vindication* contests the discourse of sexual difference, and creates a political theory that moves women from silent objects to speaking subjects' (1996: 69–70).

Wollstonecraft is remarkably contemporary in her thinking, extending the claims of Enlightenment humanism to women and also starting a debate about the relationship between sex and citizenship, thus challenging male conceptions. As Gunther-Canada (1996: 75) comments: 'Wollstonecraft's "wild wish" to confound the distinction of sex in society' gives rise to the even more 'ambitious call for women to represent themselves in government (1989, 217)'.

Gunther-Canada highlights some of the contemporary implications of Wollstonecraft's feminism. She shows that 'Wollstonecraft's *Vindication of the Rights of Men* and *A Vindication of the Rights of Woman* provide the basis for a radical examination of the relationship between theory and practice, revealing the contradictions between gender and authority' (Gunther-Canada, 1996: 76).

In addition, as Gunther-Canada (1996: 76) shows, 'they also highlight possible strategies for subverting gender categories through a critical examination of the central role that gender plays in political thought'. As is shown in Chapter Four, Wollstonecraft's establishment of a literary space and its relationship with a theory of political rights is an important feature of her work. As Gunther-Canada (1996: 76) conveys, 'she attempts to create a literary space to expound her theory of political rights by confounding the distinction of sex in discourse ... Wollstonecroft transforms the discourse of political theory as a woman writing about the political rights of women.' As a feminist, her *Vindications* 'explode eighteenth century constructions of authority and femininity' (Gunther–Canada, 1996: 77).

Is Wollstonecraft's feminism anti-woman?

While Wollstonecraft's (1792) *A Vindication of the Rights of Woman* provided a feminist critique of 18th-century philosophers, her strongest criticism came in her last novel, *Maria, or The Wrongs of Woman*. In this she indicates that these philosophers are highly critical of 'the evils which arise in society from the despotism of rank and riches', but at the same time they treat women with cruelty. In *A Vindication of the Rights of Woman*, Wollstonecraft (1792a: 90) comments: 'I may be accused of arrogance ... still I must declare what I firmly believe that all writers who have written on the subject of female education and manners from Rousseau to De Gregory, have contributed to ... degrade one half of the human species and render women pleasing at the expense of every solid virtue.'

However, Wollstonecraft is also highly critical of women for allowing 'the passions of men' to turn them into spoilt and trivial caricatures. These men, she states, have 'placed women on thrones' where she says they perch like 'caged songbirds', 'stalk[ing] with mock majesty from perch to perch'. These women are 'caressed and spoiled, such women luxuriate in their sexual reign' (Wollstonecraft, 1792a: 90).

The question is, does Wollstonecraft's feminism appear as anti-woman, and if so, why?

Taylor (2005: 44) argues that it is 'partly the "anti-elitist" thrust of her argument and her view that "middle-class gallants and coquettes are merely aping "the great"'. As Taylor observes, Wollstonecraft is uncompromising in her condemnation of 'courtly licentiousness' that provides eroticized images of women. She maintains that 'gallantry imposes on women a "sexual distinction" which is as fake as it is destructive, displacing female human beings with eroticised "fair creatures", "lovely goddesses", "angels" – "chimeras of the male imagination"' (2005: 44). Wollstonecraft (1792a: 176) summarily dismisses such images:

> Why are girls to be told that they resemble angels, ... but to sink them below women? ... Yet they are told at the same time, that they are only angels when they are young and beautiful; consequently, it is their person not their virtues,

that procure them their Homage ... happy would it be for woman, if they were only flattered by the men who loved them; I mean who love the individual, not the sex ...

Wollstonecraft argues that for women to fully benefit from the Enlightenment they must forgo the 'false femininity' foisted upon them and look to the 'practical virtues' of rationality and independence. As Taylor (2005: 44) shows, Wollstonecraft was part of a circle of radical intellectuals who frequently challenged gender norms and met regularly to have dinner as a group of public intellectuals. However, after the explicit exposé of Wollstonecraft's life by Godwin's *Memoirs* (1798) describing her sexual history, there was an outpouring of right-wing abuse, which transformed her from a respected writer and philosopher to a spokeswoman for revolutionary depravity, in which she was called a 'philosophical wanton' and a 'hyena in petticoats'.

Godwin's distress at the loss of Wollstonecraft failed to allow him to recognize the impact of his revelations on Wollstonecraft's reputation. Peltz (2008: 112) notes that

Godwin made no attempt to hide the less respectable events of Wollstonecraft's life. He shocked readers with details of how she had flung herself at a married Fuseli, had lived out of wedlock with Gilbert Imlay, by whom she had an illegitimate child, and had twice attempted suicide, had become pregnant before her marriage to Godwin and, finally had refused religious rites on her deathbed.

Women and citizenship in the work of Mary Wollstonecraft

Wollstonecraft developed her analysis of political theory through the relationship between women and citizenship and by showing, through her work, women's claims to full and equal citizenship. Lefebvre and White (2009) provide an analysis of the relationship between Wollstonecraft's writings, women and citizenship. Lefebvre and White (2009: 461) maintain that one of the contributions of *A Vindication of the Rights of Woman* to citizenship is the inherent claim that women and men have a natural and equally shared capacity for reason that, they argue, forms the basis of citizenship.

Wollstonecraft argues that any limitation that women have is the result of lack of adequate educational opportunities. Lefebvre and White (2009: 463) argue that 'It is not education narrowly conceived that is the fault of society's manners but the form it takes in combination with wealth, courtly greed and inheritance laws that produces the rise of "factitious and corrupt manners" alongside an irrelevant and problematic education (Wollstonecraft, 1995, p. 67).'

As shown above, the basis of Wollstonecraft's critique is the fact that women have not cultivated their natural-born capacity for reason. She argues that, as a result, they have succumbed to the pull of idle pleasures, unrealistic fantasy and amusing coquetry. She argues that the consequence is that women have become silly and vain, and so, she argues, 'they are weakened by false refinements that, respecting morals, their condition is much below what it would be, were they left in a state nearer to nature' (Wollstonecraft, 1995: 136, cited in Lefebvre and White, 2010).

Wollstonecraft's critique is restricted to women, but is also directed at men. As Lefebvre and White (2010: 463) comment: 'Men are also a source of discontent for they encourage vanity and self-concern by treating women as accessories and playthings rather than as equal helpmates.' In support of this contention, Wollstonecraft (1995: 74, as cited in Lefebvre and White, 2010) shows that the history of books written by men presents women as 'alluring mistresses' rather than as 'affectionate wives and rational mothers'. Wollstonecraft (1995: 229, as cited in Lefebvre and White, 2010) argues that men and women 'mutually corrupt as well as mutually approve one another'.

The first issue identified by Wollstonecraft is that both women and men have succumbed to what she regards as problematic conceptions of beauty that, she argues, valorize physical weakness and childish intelligence. Wollstonecraft (1995: 165, as cited in Lefebvre and White, 2010) maintains that if it were not for a problematic notion of beauty, 'women would acquire sufficient to enable them to earn their own subsistence, the true definition of independence'. Second, Wollstonecraft argues that what she describes as the want of chastity in men leads women into 'relations of impermanence with devastating consequences for women' (1995: 228, as cited in Lefebvre and White, 2010). She argues that men's drives are equally damaging for them, as their carnal and 'voluptuous interests' mean that they fall prey to their appetites and become distracted from the kinds of self-discipline necessary for reason.

Wollstonecraft's answer is to remove the barriers that restrict women from learning and to expose them to improvements in science, literature and philosophy. She argues that it is only through developing their minds that women will become independent and able to exercise their rights and perform their duties. As she comments, 'the only method of leading women to fulfil their peculiar duties is to free them from all restraint by allowing them to participate in the inherent rights of mankind' (Wollstonecraft, 1995: 272, as cited in Lefebvre and White, 2010).

Wollstonecraft makes some interesting and contemporary points when she says that the most potent sign of failure is that women have become persuaded by the value of weakness. Lefebvre and White (2010: 465) make some interesting points about Wollstonecraft's conceptualization of citizenship and they note that she recognises that this will change over time. She sees women's potential as ultimately dependent on the nature and extent of education.

Lefebvre and White (2010: 465) note that: 'Her ambitions are not modest: she hopes that women will eventually use their training to participate actively in society as physicians and nurses, business women and writers. But for this to happen women need to be educated alongside men in every pursuit. For again, it is only by means of an education grounded in reason that women's duties may become redefined.' By this they mean a redefinition of women's responsibilities away from the domestic sphere.

To achieve this, Wollstonecraft demands 'a revolution in female manners' (Wollstonecraft, 1995: 292, as cited in Lefebvre and White, 2010). She views women as displaying weakness in their dependence on men, which prevents women from fulfilling the basic demands of citizenship. Second, this weakness reinforces the imbalance that encourages women to use cunning and trickery to secure their ideas. Her remedy is the re-education of both sexes.

For Wollstonecraft it is through a commitment to good citizenship that humanity can realize its potential. She maintains that this is best achieved through marriage and acts as 'the cement of society' (Wollstonecraft, 1995: 149, 260, as cited in Lefebvre and White, 2010).

Wollstonecraft maintains that women need a new education to remove them from the illegitimate power that debases them. Wollstonecraft (1995: 248, as cited in Lefebvre and White, 2010) states: 'When, therefore I call women, slaves I mean in a political and civil sense; for, indirectly they obtain too much power, and are debased by their exertions to obtain illicit sway.'

Catherine Macaulay: political activist and republican

Catherine Macaulay is viewed as one of the leading political activists of her time. Her *History of England* (1763–83) was seen as a significant intellectual contribution. Peltz (2008: 96) shows that 'Even Macaulay's great political opponent, Edmund Burke ... reacting to her radical critique of his *Thoughts on the Cause of the Present Discontent* (1770) exclaimed "the virago is the[ir] greatest champion"'. Peltz also notes that while Burke here clearly intended 'a slight on both Macaulay's femininity and her radical peers, the label "virago" – a woman who acts with the power and manner of a man – tacitly recognised her masculine prowess as a political figure' (Peltz, 2008: 96).

The driving force of Macaulay's politics was not feminism but republicanism. O'Brien (2005) maintains that her historical writings were and remain a significant contribution to politics. However, she notes that Macaulay's writings do not reflect a woman's perspective, nor do they reflect anything on the 'historical progress of women'. O'Brien shows that through her methodology Macaulay made a contribution to feminist ideas as a feminist historian. As O'Brien (2005: 523) comments: 'In her histories, she modernised and refashioned classical republican ideas in such a way as to set before her readers an ideal of individual rationality, responsibility and action; ... is applicable to women as well as men.' Macaulay's networking on republicanism resonated with other women writers, including Mary Wollstonecraft (see below).

Perhaps the most scholarly and comprehensive authority on Macaulay is captured in Bridget Hill's (1992) *The Republican Virago. The Life and Times of Catherine Macaulay*. Hill (1992: 130) describes Macaulay as a 'remarkable republican historian' and shows that as a historian, a political polemicist, a 'learned lady' and fearless critic of all that she thought wrong, Macaulay broke every rule in the 18th-century book on how a woman should conduct herself and the role she should occupy. Hill (1992: 130) writes that her second marriage to a man 26 years her junior and her social inferior demonstrated her anti-establishment attitude and was an example of her rejection of what were regarded as acceptable standards of behaviour. Hill (1992: 131) notes that 'When she commenced her *History*, Catherine Macaulay was conscious of the uniqueness of her position, and of "the invidious censures which may ensue from striking into a path of literature rarely trodden by my sex".' She refused to allow these considerations to keep her 'mute in the cause of liberty and virtue' (Macaulay, 1763–83, 1: x).

As with many other women writing at the same time, Macaulay's reviewers and commentators saw her not as a historian but as a female historian. Hill (1992: 136) gives as an example the commentary of 'Samuel Badcock (1747–88), the literary critic, in his favourable review of *The Immutability of Moral Truth* in 1789, [who] wrote that it was "really wonderful considering her sex"'. And lest he should be thought 'impolite', he appealed to the ladies to acknowledge that 'in general their talents are not adapted to abstract speculation' (*Gentleman's Magazine*, 1789, 59: 777, cited in Hill, 1992: 136).

Hill (1992: 139–40) also notes that 'it was impossible for any woman in the eighteenth century to associate with a man, share his political views, or merely enjoy his company, without it being assumed that it was not politics, or intellectual interest which drew them together but that the relationship was sexual. This goes some way to accounting for the large number of men to whom Catherine Macaulay was reported married or about to be married.'

Macaulay, women and politics

Macaulay's *History*, as indicated previously, is not a history of women and is not directed at improving women's position, but Macaulay does attempt to honour the female sex when she can. The work which addressed women's issues, and predominantly their education, was *Letters on Education* (1790a). Macaulay's views on women were deeply influenced by her own experiences as a woman. Whereas Wollstonecraft wrote in more generic terms about women, Macaulay's writing reflected a more personal and specific set of circumstances. As Hill (1992: 142–3) shows:

> Catherine Macaulay knew how easily women's reputations could be destroyed, their character defamed, and their work ignored. If the position of women was better than it had been under slavery she wrote, 'we … have no great reason to boast of our privileges, or of the candour and indulgence of the men towards us'. Compared with men she admitted women, 'in point of corporal strength' demonstrated 'some degree of inferiority' but this advantage had been abused and exploited by men 'in the barbarous ages of mankind' as 'to destroy all the natural rights of the female species and reduce them to a state of abject slavery'…

However, like Wollstonecraft's, Macaulay's writing was grounded also in her views of education and linked, says Hill, to her views on gender, vice and virtue. In her *Letters on Education* she noted: 'Let your children be brought up together; let their sports and studies be the same; let them enjoy, in the constant presence of those who are set over them all that freedom which innocence renders harmless and in which Nature rejoices.' She argued that: 'The meaning of vice and virtue, ... was the same for both sexes for there was but one rule of right for the conduct of all rational beings (Macaulay, 1790: 47, 50)' (cited in Hill, 1992: 144).

Macaulay published *Letters on Education* in 1790 and Wollstonecraft reviewed the text for the radical monthly *The Analytical Review*. In *A Vindication of the Rights of Woman*, Wollstonecraft went further by advocating a system of national day schools where a trade would be taught alongside lessons in civic virtue. As Gunther-Canada (2003: 48) comments: 'She argues that no woman can be virtuous and no nation can be considered enlightened unless women are educated to think for themselves and to exercise political rights whether single, married or widowed.' Gunther-Canada also notes that Wollstonecraft's work helped to popularize Macaulay's text and that Wollstonecraft also sought to challenge the historian's assumptions on class and gender politics. Macaulay's emphasis on home-based education gave the advantage to elite females, and at the same time restricted women to the household.

While Macaulay focuses on elite education, Wollstonecraft democratizes education by advocating a national system which would give women economic skills and at the same time prepare them for both parenthood and the rights of citizenship. Gunther-Canada (2003: 49) argues that *Letters on Education* and *A Vindication of the Rights of Woman* represent acts of political imagination: 'By linking co-education to civic education, Macaulay and Wollstonecraft develop a line of reasoning that would lead to the enfranchisement of women as citizens.'

Gunther-Canada (2003: 49) points out that the model of national education outlined in *A Vindication of the Rights of Woman* was drawn on by the US suffragists Elizabeth Candy Stanton and Susan B. Anthony, who argued for women's rights. She also shows that in Macaulay's work there is an interesting distinction between the *History of England* and *Letters on Education*. In the *History*, Macaulay shows that women have not had the same opportunities as men through serving their country in the legislature or through travel. 'Thus it is surprising that in *Letters on Education* she claims that the same curriculum that creates in young men the characteristics for civic virtue is also suited to young women ... Her educational model is grounded in the fundamental belief that women are capable of abstract thought and rational beings should rule themselves' (Gunther-Canada, 2003: 49).

Gunther-Canada goes on to say that: 'Throughout the *Letters*, Catherine Macaulay champions intellectual equality and condemns the "vices and foibles which are peculiar to the female sex" that have caused women to be considered "beneath cultivation" since antiquity'

(Macaulay 1790: 209, cited in Gunther-Canada, 2003: 55). She also makes an important point in relation to the public/private dichotomy in relation to Macaulay's views on education. She notes that Macaulay's pedagogy does little to change the politics of women's situation, which keeps women in the home. 'She laments the "particular situation" of English women is characterised by "a total and absolute exclusion of every political right": but she does not attack the separation of spheres that relegate wealthy females to a domestic passivity within the household' (Gunther-Canada, 2003: 56).

In the volumes of the *History*, Macaulay discusses women solely in terms of their relationships with men, and argues that the role of women is to support male citizens in relation to republican politics. Gunther-Canada (2003: 56) notes that 'When Macaulay writes of women in politics, she judges their involvement according to a classical model of civic virtue that envisions the ideal republic as one that excludes women from the public sphere.' In fact Macaulay's position on women in politics is outlined in the third volume of her *History of England*, which is to maintain the focus on domestic matters.

Wollstonecraft, on the other hand, has a radically different perspective on female education to Macaulay's. Wollstonecraft sees education as transformative through 'a national educational policy that is geared towards creating virtuous citizens of both sexes' (Gunther-Canada, 2003: 58).

The early education of Macaulay and Wollstonecraft highlights the differences in their approach. Wollstonecraft was the daughter of a family which had experienced financial decline. She had learned to manage by herself and did not benefit from a family library of books, which Macaulay enjoyed on her father's estate. As noted by Gunther-Canada, Wollstonecraft, with particular foresight in *A Vindication of the Rights of Woman*, argues that many poor girls have lost their livelihood as traditional forms of women's work become the occupation of craftsmen.

This raises an important point, which is that Wollstonecraft considers the economic dimensions of education in *A Vindication of the Rights of Woman* but this is, as Gunther-Canada (2003: 60) states, entirely absent from Macaulay's *Letters*. 'The propertied classes that are the focus of Macaulay's volume measured their independence by not having to work for a living.' By comparison, Wollstonecraft's perspective on education was a transformative one:

> Mary Wollstonecraft's model of national education directly confronts the weakness of women's education and seeks

to transform women's situation by changing the status of wives in marriage. She would teach women a marketable skill so that they have options outside of marriage and can contribute to the economic security of their families if they choose to marry. (Gunther-Canada, 2003: 61)

As noted previously, Wollstonecraft is damning of the sexual politics of English society, maintaining that women could avoid 'prostituting' themselves in marriage if they could earn their own living and avoid reliance on their husbands. As Wollstonecraft (1792b [1988]: 218) comments, 'nor would an attempt to earn their own subsistence, a most laudable one! sink them almost to the level of those poor abandoned creatures who live by prostitution'.

Wollstonecraft, says Gunther-Canada, sees a direct correlation between education, rationality and civil rights so that women can participate in the government. But this is still with a view to making them more competent in the private sphere. As Wollstonecraft (1792b [1988]: 250) shows: 'The conclusion which I wish to draw is obvious; make women rational creatures, and free citizens, and they will quickly become good wives and mothers; that is – if men do not neglect the duties of husband and fathers.'

While Wollstonecraft borrows Macaulay's method, she radicalises the message. But what distinguishes her argument from Macaulay's in *Letters* is that Wollstonecraft rejects the unjust laws that separate women into private and public spheres and thus, in Wollstonecraft's view, 'deny women the opportunity to exercise civic virtue' (Gunther-Canada, 2003: 62). In fact, as Gunther-Canada (2003: 64) concludes, 'Wollstonecraft turned Macaulay's claim of female intellectual equality into a call for political equality in her rights tract.'

Macaulay was not primarily concerned with the position of women either politically or sexually. There is no doubt she was sympathetic to women, but neither her *History* nor her political polemic was primarily concerned with them. As Hill (1992: 146–7) shows, Macaulay recognized that 'women experienced a total and absolute exclusion from every political right (Macaulay, 1790: 210)'. However, as Hill argues, 'reform of women's representation was not one of her priorities. In so far as she believed in an extension of the franchise she thought true political equality was impossible of achievement without more education of those yet disenfranchised.'

Macaulay's confidence in her political convictions challenged conventional political norms. Hill cites the case of Macaulay in post-dinner conversation with men: 'The Reverend Joseph Price, a

near neighbour and friend of John Sawbridge noted on dining ...
"Mrs Macaulay does not retire after dinner with the ladies, but stays
with the men" [Price, Ditchfield and Lucas, 1991: 141]' (Hill, 1992:
147–8).

Macaulay and the politics of republicanism

As noted, Macaulay's work was well received in the US and Benjamin
Franklin was an admirer of her *History* and purchased the eight-
volume work to include it in the University of Virginia library. In
fact, Macaulay first came to national prominence in her thirties with
the publication of the first volume of her *History of England* (1763),
which covered the history of the early 17th century. In addition to
seven more volumes over the next 20 years, she also wrote pamphlets
on the subject of electoral reform, constitutional theory and, in 1775,
the crisis in America. Macaulay was acquainted with leading radical
intellectuals in Britain, France and America and she mixed with
activists for constitutional reform, such as John Wilkes, members of the
Society for the Support of the Bill of Rights and republican political
theorists (Hill, 1992). It is very clear, as O'Brien (2005) notes, that
republicanism took priority over gender.

The relationship between gender, nationality and history was gaining
wider circulation when Macaulay was writing the final volumes of the
History. O'Brien (2005: 534) comments: 'The progressive feminisation
of patriotism in this period formed the basis of many women's claims
to write authoritatively of history and nation. Yet there is no trace of
the idea of a specifically female patriotism in her work.'

Mary Wollstonecraft and Catherine Macaulay:
convergences and contradictions

The relationship between Catherine Macaulay and Mary Wollstonecraft
is one that has interested historians, and Frazer (2011: 605) maintains
that Macaulay's work had a direct influence on Wollstonecraft and that
'the ideas that infuse their thinking, are very much part of the general
heritage of progressive oppositional eighteenth century intellectual
culture'.

In an article entitled 'The Links Between Mary Wollstonecraft and
Catherine Macaulay: New Evidence', Hill (1995) argues that recently
found letters highlight the fact that Wollstonecraft and Macaulay did
in fact have minimal correspondence with one another. Hill argues
that this emerged from the responses of both to Edmund Burke's

Reflections on the Revolution in France. Hill (1995: 177) argues that 'the two women were remarkably close in their ideas on democracy, equality and women's rights – ideas ultimately circumscribed by eighteenth century radicals' notions of property and class'.

As shown in the correspondence quoted at the outset of this chapter, in December 1790 Mary Wollstonecraft wrote to Catherine Macaulay indicating that they shared a similarity of views. Catherine Macaulay responds to Wollstonecraft by thanking her for the pamphlet that Wollstonecraft has sent her, and is flattering of Wollstonecraft's work; and Macaulay sends Wollstonecraft her notes on Edmund Burke. Wollstonecraft is also very flattering of Macaulay's work in *A Vindication of the Rights of Woman.*

Hill (1995: 179) states that these were two women public intellectuals who devoted a large part of their lives to writing at a time 'when learning in the female sex was largely abhorred'. Wollstonecraft wrote more directly about the position of women, although, as Hill points out, a few years before her death Macaulay devoted part of her *Letters on Education* to the subject. Both women visited France and expressed great admiration for the French Revolution.

Both wrote responses to Burke's *Reflections on the Revolution in France* – Mary Wollstonecraft in *A Vindication of the Rights of Men* (1790), and Catherine Macaulay in *Observations on the Reflections of the Rt. Hon. Edmund Burke on the Revolution in France* (1790b). Both also were passionately concerned with the education of women and children and wrote books on the theme: Mary Wollstonecraft (1787) *Thoughts on the Education of Daughters* and Catherine Macaulay (1790) *Letters on Education with Observations on Religious and Metaphysical Subjects.*

On the issue of education, Macaulay and Wollstonecraft were influenced by philosophers such as Hobbes and Burke, and Wollstonecraft shares a good deal of Macaulay's critical reading of Rousseau on education. Frazer (2011: 603) maintains that 'Their method of criticism, as well as their developed evaluations of equality and friendship, are notably significant for later feminists and social theory …'

Frazer highlights the parallels and differences between Macaulay and Wollstonecraft. In 1790, Wollstonecraft was 31, a published author as well as an editor and translator, and had experience of running a school and as a governess in an aristocratic household. She mixed in radical and dissenting circles formed by her publisher, Joseph Johnson, in central London.

Macaulay, by contrast, had a more international appeal and her work was celebrated in North America and Paris. However, by 1780 (as was shown earlier) Macaulay's 'reputation had suffered from the pitfalls of celebrity culture' (Frazer, 2011: 604). As Frazer shows, 'As aspects of her family life were lampooned, her reputation and power as a Whig propagandist receded and the later volumes of her *History* were not the best sellers that the earlier ones are.'

Frazer (2011: 604) shows that the December 1790 issue of the *Analytical Review* included reviews of both Wollstonecraft's *Vindication* and Macaulay's *Observations on the Reflections of the Rt. Hon Edmund Burke on the Revolution in France*. In November 1790 the *Analytical Review* had published an admiring review by Wollstonecraft of Macaulay's *Letters on Education* (1790). Wollstonecraft and Macaulay were in private communication at this time, although they never met (see Hill, 1995).

Wollstonecraft and Macaulay: activism and republicanism

Macaulay was more of a political activist and republican than Wollstonecraft was, and more involved in day-to-day practical politics. Hill (1995: 181) shows that both Wollstonecraft and Macaulay were self-taught. Macaulay never attended a school and relied on a private education by a governess and her father's library. Wollstonecraft received meagre education. Both women were influenced by dissent, and both welcomed the French Revolution.

In her letter to Catherine Macaulay, Mary Wollstonecraft included a copy of the *Vindication of the Rights of Men* (1790). In her reply Catherine Macaulay praised Wollstonecraft and sent a copy of her *Observations on the Reflections of the Rt. Hon. Edmund Burke on the Revolution in France*.

Hill maintains that Wollstonecraft's critique of Burke was about 'rights', and states that, in response to Burke's argument that liberties are derived from our 'forefathers', Wollstonecraft wrote that such liberties were 'rights which men inherit at their birth, as rational creatures – not from their forefathers but from God, [and] prescription can never undermine natural rights' (Hill, 1995: 183).

While Wollstonecraft and Macaulay did share a great deal intellectually, Hill (1995: 184) shows that 'one thing that did separate the two works and indeed the two women in their radicalism – is that Wollstonecraft was in no doubt why such liberty – the birthright of man – had never been achieved. It was, she wrote, "the demon of property" which had encroached "on the sacred rights of men" [*The Analytical Review* (1790) VIII: 419–421]' (cited in Hill, 1995: 184). Wollstonecraft was also more sympathetic to the poor than was Macaulay, who did not identify with the poor or dispossessed as Wollstonecraft did. Macaulay did not reject property rights and she argued that liberty involved the security of property, even though it was clear that this could be abused by the wealthy and powerful. Macaulay never raised the issue of women's suffrage and she argued that lack of education made real political inequality impossible.

Working-class women and women's suffrage

Both Macaulay and Wollstonecraft had reservations about 'lower-class' women taking the political initiative. Hill (1995: 185) shows that Wollstonecraft's position on the revolution in France had changed as the revolution became increasingly anarchic: 'For Wollstonecraft the final years in revolutionary France after the Terror had begun were to be a disillusionary experience and she was to move closer to Burke's condemnation of Paris market women.'

> 'No-one', it's been said of her, 'was more afraid of the revolutionary crowd' [Hutton, 1992: 23, n23]. The women who marched to Versailles were now 'rabble' and the 'lowest refuse of the streets, women who had thrown off the virtues of one sex without having the power to assume more than the vices of the other' [Wollstonecraft, 1794: 196–7]. (Hill, 1995: 185)

Hill (1995: 185) notes that in Wollstonecraft's analysis of the French Revolution she made no suggestion of the importance of women's involvement or of their achievements. In addition, she also came to share Macaulay's reservations about lower-class women taking the political initiative and, as Hill shows, she came increasingly to see that the political rights of women were really only for women of the 'propertied classes', whom she called 'women of a superior cast'.

Hill shows that when Wollstonecraft returned from France she had moved much closer to Macaulay's views, and notes that 'In their failure to pursue equal political rights for women Macaulay and Wollstonecraft were in no way exceptional among eighteenth-century radicals who were "not prepared to extend the suffrage to women because they regarded women as incapable of exercising a free rational and independent choice" [Todd and Butler, 1989: 21]' (Hill, 1995: 185).

Hill (1995: 186) indicates that 'the most important difference between the two women was that Wollstonecraft had herself early

experienced poverty and deprivation. She had had to work for a living
– something Macaulay was never called on to do – and been forced
to confront the difficulties facing intelligent self-educated women
of the middle-class in their search for employment.' Wollstonecraft
thought that it was important that women should work and become
independent. While less of a political activist in conventional terms
than Macaulay, she was more engaged in the practical politics of
everyday life and was aware of social tensions between rich and poor.

In her final work, *A Vindication of the Rights of Woman* (1792),
Wollstonecraft shows her debt to Macaulay's *Letters on Education* (1790).
In it Wollstonecraft was to repeat much of Macaulay's argument that
she rejected education for women that was simply aimed at making
them 'more attractive companions for men' (Wollstonecraft, 1792a:
59). But she went further and argued that education should make
them 'independent and useful to society' (Wollstonecraft, 1792a: 59).

Scandal and satire in the lives of Wollstonecraft and Macaulay

Both Macaulay and Wollstonecraft were the subject of scandal as a
result of their relationships and marriages. They were also the subject
of vicious satire and attacks by the literati – both women and men.

In the case of Macaulay, members of the conservative bluestockings
were highly critical of her work and her behaviour. Hannah More
wrote to Mrs Boscawen as follows: 'This woman [...] is far from
being any criterion by which to judge the whole sex; she was not
feminine either in her writings or her manners; she was only a tolerable
cleverman' (1925: 80, cited in Hill, 1992: 144).

Hill (1992: 144) notes that there was rivalry and envy between the two
writers, with More being envious of Macaulay. More not only disliked
Catherine Macaulay, but had a horror, says Hill, of female politicians, and
disliked those who meddled in politics. Hill also notes that while other
members of the bluestockings were less vindictive in their prejudices, they
too shared the belief that politics was not a sphere in which women should
interfere, and they were particularly dismissive about Macaulay's brand
of politics. Hill observes that Elizabeth Montagu refused to read any of
Macaulay's writings. More claimed that as a result of her second marriage,
Macaulay had broken the rules of strict morality and should be shunned.

The political schisms between the conservative bluestockings such as
Montagu and More and Macaulay and Wollstonecraft were significant,
with Montagu engaging in sexist and moralistic commentary. Montagu
maintained that Macaulay's politics made her *History* unreadable,

and she was also critical of what she saw as Macaulay's violation of gender boundaries. Montagu claimed that 'All this happened from her adopting masculine opinions and masculine manners. "I hate a woman's mind in men's cloaths ... I always look'd upon Mrs Macaulay as rather belonging to the lads ... than as one of the gentle sex. Indeed she was always a strange fellow"' (cited in Peltz, 2008: 104).

The personal lives of Macaulay and Wollstonecraft were both the subject of considerable ridicule and satire. Peltz (2008: 96) maintains that Macaulay's increasingly flamboyant life in Bath was centred on 'her unconventional living arrangements with her admirer the Reverend Thomas Wilson ... who was nearly thirty years her senior. Although Macaulay was undoubtedly attracted to his library, his intellectual company and his partisan politics, many assumed her motives were less pure.'

Peltz (2008: 100) shows how Macaulay's relationship was 'first satirized in the *Town and Country Magazine* in its "Tete-a-Tete" series', which usually brought public attention to illicit romantic liaisons between society figures. Peltz notes that the Tete-a-Tete series was published between 1762 and 1792 and that 'while the format of the illustrations consciously emulated marriage portraits or miniatures exchanged by lovers, the pairings were often rather more scurrilous or cynical than first appeared' (2008: 100).

She comments that the portrait of Wilson and Macaulay, which was a satirization of their relationship, was entitled 'The Political Platonic Lovers', and of course made imputations of sexual impropriety.

The satirization of Macaulay's relationship was not restricted to the *Town and County Magazine*, but was also lampooned in *A Speedy and Effectual Preparation for the Next World*, another satirical illustration. In the latter, Peltz (2008: 101) states that the satire attacks 'Macaulay's inflated vanity ... which was the result of having her head turned by extensive flattery and her consequent assumption that she was somehow above normal behaviour'. The level of satire was deeply sexist and ageist, as well as vicious. Peltz states that *A Speedy and Effectual Preparation* develops the theme of vanity by representing Macaulay as a deluded old widow with an unseemly interest in cosmetics and fashion. Macaulay is represented as seated at her dressing table, 'her ludicrous tall hair bedecked with a hearse, drawn by a plumed horses'. As Peltz (2008: 101) continues: 'Like so many fashion satires of the period, this mocks the "present mode for dressing the head" that Hannah More deemed "absurd, extravagant and fantastical" [Roberts, 1834: 51].'

Peltz (2008: 101) also shows that even 'rouge' had implications, and she argues that the '"rouge" that Macaulay applies was also emotive.

It was filled with nationalist and sexual symbolism because make-up was equated with French manners and the perversion of "natural" and polite femininity.' Peltz indicates that even Macaulay's health was seen as a source of satire and refers to the illness she suffered while writing the fifth volume of her *History*. Her doctor, James Graham, had published a long letter regarding her treatment and Thomas Wilson 'threw a lavish and theatrical birthday party to celebrate her recovery. An account of the festivities was given to the press.' Peltz also notes that, despite her close relationship with Thomas Wilson, Macaulay added further to her flamboyant reputation by suddenly marrying William Graham, who was the 21-year-old brother of her physician.

Peltz (2008: 104) comments that 'The prospects of this 47 year old historian and champion of the republican cause marrying a poorly educated shipsmate less than half her age had had predictable consequences in polite society. A plethora of salacious satires, both literary and graphic, delighted in exposing the marriage as an abomination.'

Another satire, *The Auspicious Marriage*, shows the 'overdressed and towering figure of Macaulay – her height exaggerated by her plumed headdress decorated with a fool's cap – ... juxtaposed with the diminutive and childlike Graham, who leads her to the altar' (Peltz, 2008: 104). This was one of several satires that all seemed to revel in Macaulay's struggle with ambition.

As shown above, in Wollstonecraft's case, the publication of her partner William Godwin's *Memoirs* in 1793, with its detailed and uncensored account of Wollstonecraft's sexual history, led to a transformation of her character by right-wing commentators, which led to an attack on her reputation.

Conclusion

The significance of Macaulay and Wollstonecraft in terms of their contribution and legacy cannot be overstated. Frazer (2011: 613–14) maintains that 'the *Vindication of the Rights of Woman* is a book that is centered in the late eighteenth century tradition of republicanism, and rights theory, is steeped in theology, is a seminal contribution to feminist philosophy and ethics, contains an outline of prescriptive political theory, ... and makes a distinctive and lastingly significant contribution to social theory'. In addition, she notes that Macaulay's work had a direct influence on Wollstonecraft and that 'the ideas that infuse their thinking, are very much part of a general heritage of progressive oppositional eighteenth century intellectual culture'

(Frazer, 2011: 605). The implications of the radicalism of Macaulay and Wollstonecraft can be seen in the later writing by women (see Chapter Four) and in subsequent social movements leading to the emergence of women as public intellectuals.

FOUR

Women writers: setting the terms of the debate

Bookish women who flaunt their erudition are singled out for attack, as they were in most modernist writings on women. Animus against learned women particularly those displaying their wisdom in print was a long-standing feature of British intellectual life that few Enlightenment writers sought to challenge. ...

[U]ntil recently historians of gender were agreed in depicting the eighteenth century as a time of hardening gender divisions, a period when men and women's lives bifurcated into separate spheres. But closer examination of the evidence, by among others, Amanda Vickery, Margaret Hunt, Linda Colley and Olwen Hutton – shows that far from becoming more entrenched, by the second half of the century, the boundaries separating men and women were ... unstable and becoming more so. (Taylor, 2005: 39)

Introduction

As indicated in previous chapters of the book, many women in the Bluestocking Circle were established writers in their own right in the 18th century. Other writers, while associated with the bluestockings, were not seen as part of the bluestockings. All contributed to the emergence of women as public intellectuals. Interestingly, the personal (private) and public (political) intersected in their lives quite profoundly and impacted on their writing. This chapter explores the idea of the bluestockings and other writers and how they were partially enfranchised by the expansion of print culture in the 18th century.

Women writers in the 17th and 18th centuries

In the 18th century, women throughout Europe in large numbers became involved in an expansive world of learning and engaged in the public exchange of ideas. Hesse (2005a: 259) points out that 'the number of women writers in France trebled to over 300 in print in the revolutionary decade alone'. In addition, Goodman (1995a) comments that 'The number of women publishing in the German speaking states quadrupled over the course of the eighteenth century, provoking Friedrich Schiller to write to Goethe in 1797 that he was "truly astounded how our women today are capable … of creating themselves as artful writers".'

Interestingly, Hesse (2005a) expands on the range of institutional contexts where women were represented and in which they articulated their views. These included Masonic lodges, which, she argues, were cosmopolitan in nature and could be found throughout Europe (Jacobus, 1991). Hesse also identifies other mixed-sex intellectual settings that she shows diverged along national, cultural and religious lines. As she comments: 'In France, salons were spaces of hetero-social exchange from their inception in the early seventeenth century, whereas in England drawing room conversation was only de-segregated in the latter half of the eighteenth century' (Hesse, 2005a: 259).

Hesse also notes that in France and Italy academies and learned societies offered at least honorific membership to women and allowed their attendance from the early years of the 18th century. However, she observes that in Protestant countries men were more hesitant to admit women.

The following summary provides a synopsis of some of the key writers from the 18th century and considers their contribution to the evolution of women as public intellectuals contributing to both writing and ideas.

Fanny Burney (1752–1840) was a popular novelist during the late 18th century. She had to overcome her family's disapproval in order to establish herself in English literary circles. She had no formal education, and despite the fact her father was a musicologist he discouraged his daughter's aspirations. Regardless of this, she was widely read and published a lot of plays and stories at a young age – but burned them all because of pressure from her family. However, she refused to allow herself to be deterred and published her first novel in 1768, *Evelina*, which was very successful. After publishing this novel she not only gained approval from her father but also got the support of Dr Samuel Johnson. She went on to become a member of Queen Charlotte's court and to secure a place in English literary society. Burney's novels focus on women's role in relation to the British aristocracy in the realms of marriage, wealth and power.

Her writings influenced other writers, such as Jane Austen. Burney's second novel, *Cecilia or Memoirs of an Heiress, By the Author of Evelina* (1782), presents a heroine who, in order to save her inheritance from her guardians, must marry a man who will adopt her name. Her work is interesting methodologically, as Burney abandons the usual letter-writing form and uses authorial narration, becoming one of the first novelists to use free indirect speech.

Burney's fourth novel, *Camilla or a Picture of Youth by the Author of Evelina and Cecilia*, involves the courtship of light-hearted Camilla by Edgar. She presents an interesting reversal of usual courtship rituals in that Edgar suffers jealousy and misapprehension because Camilla has been advised by her father not to express her feelings.

Elizabeth Carter (1717–1806) was a prominent member of the bluestockings and was seen as one of the most scholarly members of the blues. She was well known for her translations, poetry, essays and letter writing. She was educated by her father, the perpetual curate of Deal, alongside her brothers and received a good education that involved a knowledge of several languages, including Latin, Greek, Hebrew, French, Italian, Spanish and German. Her father was Edward Cave, editor of *The Gentleman's Magazine*, who began to publish Carter's work in his periodical. Carter moved in English literary circles and developed friendships with Samuel Johnson, Catherine Talbot, Elizabeth Montagu, Samuel Richardson, Edmund Burke, Horace Walpole and Hannah More.

Elizabeth Robinson Montagu (1720–1800) was another leading member of the bluestockings and in fact was known as 'Queen of the Bluestockings'. She was the sister of the novelist Sarah Scott and was very active in literary circles. She was educated at home and widely read. As shown in Chapter One, she was a central figure in promoting literary and intellectual exchanges. Her gatherings held in her various houses were attended by a host of literary luminaries, including Samuel Johnson, Hester Thrale, David Garrick, Edmund Burke and Horace Walpole. In her famous *Essay on the Writings and Genius of Shakespear* she defends Shakespeare against Voltaire by comparing him with French and Greek dramatists and establishes Shakespeare as a figure of national pride.

Another interesting woman writer with an unorthodox personal life was Lady Mary Wortley Montagu (1689–1762). She was the cousin of Henry Fielding and had an aristocratic family. She eloped with Edward Wortley, who served as ambassador to Turkey, where she wrote *Turkish Embassy Letters* (1716–18). Her elopement with Edward Wortley resulted from the collapse of a financial arrangement around their marriage. She wrote *An Essay on the Mischief of Giving Fortunes with Women in Marriage* recommending the abolition of the marriage dowry. While her husband was ambassador, Mary Wortley did a lot of sightseeing and touring in Turkey. After her return to London Alexander Pope had a portrait painted of her in Turkish dress.

As with a number of prominent women writers and thinkers, Mary Wortley's personal life led to the development of a reputation that Desai (1993: xx) describes as corrupt and scandalous. Despite this, she remained well regarded and Voltaire asked her to comment on a manuscript of epic poetry. When she was 47 she became infatuated with an Italian student, Francesco Algarotti, to whom, as Desai comments, she wrote passionate letters. She persuaded her husband that she needed a change of air and went to join Algarotti in Italy in 1739. She was never to see her husband again and returned to England only to die. Desai (1993: xxi) notes that

> her romance was revealed when Lord Byron came upon some letters of hers in Venice and sent them to his publisher, John Murray, in 1818. Not that there was much to reveal for the romance turned out to be largely a figment of Lady Mary's imagination. Algarotti had found himself a patron, and possibly a lover – in the Crown Prince Frederick of Prussia – who addressed him as 'The Swan of Padua' [in Halsband, 1956: 184] and she did not see him until March 1741 when they spent two weeks together in Turin.

Desai (1993: xxv) states that Mary Wortley left two volumes of her Turkish letters with the Reverend Benjamin Snowden, minister of Rotterdam. *The Embassy Letters* are the best known of her published works. Her daughter and son-in-law bought the manuscript from the Reverend Snowden for £500 and it appeared in *The London Chronicle* in 1763. She returned to England in 1762 after an absence of 23 years and died of cancer the same year.

Desai (1993: xxv) provides some interesting insight into Mary Wortley's writing:

> The letters reveal a great anxiety to stress that the society Lady Mary moved in was 'of the first quality', the houses she visited belonged to 'people of quality', even the nuns she met were 'all of quality'. She repeatedly pointed out that previous travellers had not come in contact with such society and therefore remained ignorant of its superior civilization, basing their accounts on encounters with the common people. The customs, culture, dress and art she praised so highly were the attributes only of the

upper class and not revealed in those whose contact was confined to the poor and the negligible with whom she was not concerned.

Lady Mary proved a traveller of 'a very diligent curiosity' [Vienna, 10 October 1716], and the reason why the *Embassy Letters* have survived ... may be that travelling to the East she was able to break away from rigid confinements – mental and intellectual as much as physical – of her own society, and showed herself exceptionally open to new impressions and points of view. This gives her letters an immediacy and vivacity that remain as fresh as the mosaics on the ancient monuments she saw and the eastern gardens that gave her such delight.

Desai comments that Mary Wortley proved to be a traveller of 'very diligent curiosity' and argues that the reason why *The Embassy Letters* have survived could be that, travelling to a country like Turkey, she was able to escape the mental, intellectual and physical confinements of her own society. She was very open to new impressions. Despite this, Desai (1993: xxvi) notes she could be 'scathing about foreign ways':

she tended to compare all she saw with what she had left behind in England, and she could be scathing of foreign ways: Viennese housing shocked her, apartments of the nobility 'divided but by partition from that of a taylor or a shoemaker' and the great stairs ... 'as common and dirty as the streets'. [Vienna, 8 September 1716]

Hannah More (1745–1833) was one of the most well-respected, prolific and widely read writers of her time. She was educated as a schoolmistress and wrote for a children's market initially. She was part of Samuel Johnson's circle and was a committed social and religious reformer, establishing Sunday schools for the poor. Her only novel was *Coelebs in Search of a Wife*. She never married and died friendless and alone.

Sarah Pennington (1783) was another woman writer who showed that the personal could intersect with the public (political). She began writing after a public and painful separation from her husband, Joseph Pennington, and their children. Interestingly, it is reported that Sarah was behaving like 'a coquette'. Her publications are somewhat autobiographical and remorseful. Her most popular publication was *An Unfortunate Mother's Advice to Her Absent Daughters in the Letter to*

Miss Pennington, which was released in 1761 and was published seven more times until 1800.

Hester Lynch Thrale Piozzi (1741–1821) was born into the English aristocracy and well educated. She was forced into an oppressive marriage and had 12 children. She met Samuel Johnson in 1765 and helped him with the translation of Boethius. She was introduced to a range of well-known public and literary figures. After her husband's death, she chose to marry an Italian Catholic, Gabriel Piozzi. This alienated Johnson, who opposed the marriage. Piozzi travelled on the Continent and settled in Wales, becoming a prolific writer of histories, travel accounts and poetry. Her best-known work is *Anecdotes* (1786), considered to be one of the most authoritative accounts of Johnson's life.

Sarah Scott (1723–95) was the elder sister to Elizabeth Montagu and was, like Elizabeth, exposed to the value of education. She was unhappily married to George Lewis Scott and left the marriage and became involved in charity work and writing. She was associated with the bluestockings and tried to establish a 'utopian community' with her sister Elizabeth. Her most famous work was the novel *A Description of Millenium Hall and the Country Adjacent*, in which she idealizes her utopian society. Her novels sold well, although she lost popularity in the 19th century.

Jane Austen's (1755–1817) work in its scope is beyond the remit of this book, but her contribution, set among the middle class as opposed to the aristocracy, established a more broadly based forum for the development of women as public intellectuals.

Austen was educated by her father and older brothers and her own self-education. She developed as a professional writer, and from 1811 to 1816 she published *Sense and Sensibility* (1811), *Pride and Prejudice* (1813), *Mansfield Park* (1814) and *Emma* (1815). Two further novels, *Northanger Abbey* and *Persuasion*, were both published in 1818.

Austen's work was published anonymously in the first instance; gradually it gained greater exposure and she became more widely accepted as a significant writer. Her work was also published by her family after her death and reflects the fact that the family wanted her to be presented in an uncontentious light. Despite the venomous critique offered by Romantics to the work of Wollstonecraft, Macaulay and the bluestockings, Austen was sympathetic with a number of the British Romantic poets, including Wordsworth, Coleridge, Keats and Byron.

Both Jane Austen and her sister Cassandra were educated initially in Oxford by a tutor, then returned home to be schooled by the family, as they could not afford not afford to school their daughters elsewhere. They had access to their father's library and the family provided an environment of open intellectual debate. Jane lived in a family environment for the rest of her life.

Jane Austen's novels were well received and she earned a regular income from her publications. She became ill in 1817 and died before the publication of *Persuasion* and *Northanger Abbey*. Cassandra and her brother Henry organized the posthumous publication of these last two books. In 1832 the publisher Richard Bentley purchased the remaining copyright of all Austen's novels and, beginning in 1832, published them in five illustrated volumes as part of his Standard Novels series. In October 1833 Bentley published the first collected edition of Austen's work. Her work has of course remained in print and has also been made into films. Austen was an important public intellectual and provided early commentary on the nature of relationships.

Bluestockings as published writers

Most of the bluestockings were published writers. Montagu (1769) published *An Essay on the Writings and Genius of Shakespear, Compared with the Greek and French Dramatic Poets, with Some Remarks upon the misrepresentation of Mons. De Voltaire*; her sister Sarah Scott (1762) wrote a *Description of Millenium Hall and the Country Adjacent*. The published works of others include Carter's (1758) *All the Works of Epictetus*, Hannah More's (1786) *The Bas Bleu*, Hester Chapone's (1773) *Letters on the Improvement of the Mind* and Eliza Haywood's (1744) periodical *Female Spectator*. Eger (2008: 48) notes that 'Haywood's periodical covered a wide range of subjects including politics, science, fashion, literary criticism and social analysis (especially of courtship and marriage), and conjured up a group of intelligent, engaged women as contributors, readers and discussants.' Eger also notes that Montagu and Carter showed that women could succeed in areas traditionally defined as ones where men excelled. Montagu was celebrated as a woman writer who challenged Voltaire's notorious criticism of Shakespeare.

Outside of the immediate 'Bluestocking Circle', 18th-century radicals such as Catherine Macaulay and Mary Wollstonecraft were also well regarded and established writers (see Chapter Three). Macaulay's *History of England* in eight volumes was recognized by key political figures such as Benjamin Franklin, who bought the eight volumes and included them in the University of Virginia library. Wollstonecraft's (1792) *A Vindication of the Rights of Woman* made explicit claims for the rights of women to full citizenship.

The movement from bluestockings as 'learned ladies' to 'cosmopolitan intellectuals' is charted by Kelly (2001). He frames the changes in terms of their intervention into traditional patriarchal culture by showing how the 'Bluestocking Circle sought to remodel intellectual culture in order that women could achieve participation' (Eger, 2001: 15). Kelly argues that they encouraged the movement towards 'the advancement of moral virtue' and 'gentry capitalism' and shows how the bluestockings pushed the boundaries of 'intellectual exchange and self-fashioning led to an experimentation of literary forms which has not received adequate recognition' (Eger, 2001: 15).

As indicated previously, the idea of a 'monolithic patriarchal culture' as characterizing the Enlightenment was not an accurate reflection of women's role in Enlightenment culture. As Eger (2008: 142) indicates, both Elizabeth Carter and Elizabeth Montagu showed in their writing that women could succeed in areas where men had traditionally excelled. Both Carter and Montagu wrote scholarly publications – Carter's *All the Works of Epictetus* (1758) and Montagu's *An Essay on the Writings and Genius of Shakespear* (1769). Carter was regarded as a scholar and Montagu was celebrated among her contemporaries as challenging Voltaire's criticism of Shakespeare. Montagu's critique of Voltaire was seen as a patriotic statement.

Apart from Carter and Montagu, there were poets like Hannah More, whose verses were acclaimed by Walpole. Hesse (2005a: 261) shows that most of the bluestockings as women of letters came from 'the upper ranks of European society: high court society, the landed gentry, the professions or the burgeoning ranks of royal officialdom throughout Europe'.

Elsewhere Eger shows how Hannah More's *The Bas Bleu* or *Conversation* was published in 1786 by Horace Walpole's Strawberry Hill printing press. Eger describes her poem 'as a celebratory memorial of a particular intellectual community which was formed in the 1750s around the prominent hostesses Elizabeth Montagu, Elizabeth Vesey and Frances Boscawen' (Eger, 2005: 288). However, as Eger (2005: 289) shows, the poem 'reflects the association of women with civilisation which was an eighteenth century idea and differed from previous associations of woman and nature'. She also shows that 'the philosophers of the Scottish Enlightenment, placed a new emphasis on the morally superior nature of women in accounts of the progress of man. The female emerged as a vital element in contemporary attempts to moralise the public sphere' (Eger, 2005: 289). Regardless of this, Eger notes that women were still restricted in what they could discuss and that women's engagement in rational discourse was frowned upon, despite the scholarship evident in the work of Montagu, Carter and More.

While the bluestockings did not define entirely new genres in terms of women's writing, their work did show a particular emphasis that Kelly (2005) maintains received literary expression in Sarah Scott's *A Description of Millenium Hall* (1762). Kelly (2015: 186–7) shows that the novel 'gave comprehensive literary expression to this gynocentric modernity ... depicting a community of women, refugees from courtly upper-class exploitation of women, pursuing learning and the arts within a program of social and economic philanthropic modernization on an estate previously ruined by extremes of upper-class extravagance and miserliness'.

An interesting point raised by Kelly (2015: 187) is that the extensive correspondence in the form of collections of letters between members of the bluestockings was frequently edited by male family members after the women died, which resulted in a more 'domestic' version of the women's work as an acceptable 'literary lady'. This can be seen in Matthew Montagu Pennington's *Letters of Elizabeth Montagu* (1809) and Pennington's letters from Talbot to Vesey (1809) and from Carter to Montagu (1817). The editing of these collections of letters 'seemed designed to counter memoirs of scandalous or political women, especially French, in the Revolutionary or Napoleonic aftermath'. As Kelly (2015: 188) shows: 'Such works enabled construction for nineteenth and early twentieth-century gentrified middle-class culture of a specifically English figure of the cultivated, perhaps learned, and occasionally heroic, yet fundamentally domestic woman.'

Eger (2005) identifies a number of the bluestockings and others, including Mary Wollstonecraft, Hannah More, Charlotte Smith, Elizabeth Inchbald and Elizabeth Carter, all of whom relied on their literary earnings, but also, by the views they expressed through their writing, on their need to establish independence. Catherine Macaulay's pamphlet *A Modest Plea for the Protection of Copyright* (1774) makes explicit the 'links between the professionalization of writing and the emergence of a middle-class increasingly determined to assert independence' (Eger, 2001: 14). Eger (2001: 14) states that Macaulay argues for a 'perpetual copyright partly on the grounds that otherwise "... independent men not born of estates will be prevented from using their talents for the benefit of mankind" and none should write except "men in opulence, and men in dependence"' (Macaulay, 1774: 37; cited in Eger).

Women writers did more than just write: they could also manipulate public opinion. An example of this is found in Eliza Haywood's writing in the journal *The Female Spectator* (1748). Her writing shows that women were not just the object of public opinion but were the subject, object and predicators of gossip. As editor of *The Female Spectator*, Haywood was aware of the necessity of balancing instruction and entertainment in catering for the readership. 'Although women who were deemed to have transgressed their proper social boundaries were often the targets of satire and gossip, in different contexts, representations of women served to symbolise the civilising influence of cultural exchange, and thus their centrality in the progress of culture' (Eger, 2005: 10).

Radical thinkers in print: Wollstonecraft and Macaulay

As shown in Chapter Three, Wollstonecraft and Macaulay were regarded as two of the most radical political theorists of the 18th century and, while the focus of their work was different, they contributed to the professionalization of women as writers, as well as making a significant contribution to the emergence of women as public intellectuals.

In order to achieve success in this context, Wollstonecraft proposed that women need to be given the necessary learning and knowledge to acquire the capacity for the development of critical and reflexive thought in order to sustain the development of a 'domestic' and national identity as required in a modern nation-state. Kelly (2015: 195) claims that Wollstonecraft uses the development of the novel form as in *Maria, or The Wrongs of Woman* for the purpose of learning and social, economic and legal research. She had previously experimented with the novel form in *Mary: A Fiction* (1788).

Beyond this, Kelly (2015: 195) shows how *The Wrongs of Woman* was an even more innovative experiment:

> *The Wrongs of Woman* was even more innovative, responding to the ideas, issues, politics, and personalities of the Revolutionary 1790s and aiming to popularize late Enlightenment critique of the Old Order, radicalize socio-cultural sentimental literary themes and techniques, and fictionalize factual instances of the wrongs of women of all classes past and present.

In addition, Kelly (2015: 197) notes:

> The argument of *The Wrongs of Woman* also rejected the advice in female conduct books that women endure

passively the inevitable ills of marriage, and reversed a corresponding and common depiction in sentimental and Gothic novels of passive heroines suffering repeated trials of mind, body and feelings.

Kelly observes that *The Wrongs of Woman* implicitly rejected the increasingly widely held view that the increasingly despotic nature of the French Revolution demonstrated the futility of modernization. Wollstonecraft died before she could provide definitive closure. The book was the culmination of a decade of her reflections across a variety of genres on the relationship of gender, class, knowledge and work in relation to modernization.

Caine (1997: 38) also shows that Wollstonecraft's *The Wrongs of Woman* represents her disillusionment with the French Revolution both in terms of its general democratic potential and in relation to the emancipatory potential for women. It is represented in the attempts to escape from madness within marriage and become emancipated, and is regarded as her most significant feminist work.

Wollstonecraft broadens her feminist philosophy in *The Vindication of the Rights of Woman*. Gunther-Canada (1996: 63) maintains that: '*The Rights of Woman* links the textual representation of women as sexual beings devoid of reason to the silence of women in the discourses that shape their lives. Wollstonecraft thus skilfully unites philosophical argument with discursive strategy to articulate a theory of women's rights.'

In addition, *A Vindication* also challenges misogynistic forms of late 18th-century political writing encapsulated in the philosophical work of writers such as Edmund Burke. As Gunther-Canada (1996: 65–6) comments: 'For Burke, the French Revolution represents an open assault on sexual hierarchy, as well as on monarchical politics ... for Burke gender uncertainty is the true horror of revolution.' In commenting on Burke, Sapiro (1992) argues that: 'Burke effectively employs the language of the sublime to evoke his powerful reaction to the class-mixing and gender-blending of the French Revolution' (cited in Gunther-Canada, 1996: 65–6).

Wollstonecraft has been criticized for using a somewhat masculine discourse in *A Vindication*, which might be seen as contradictory, given the feminist philosophical position adopted. Taylor (2005: 30) cites Wollstonecraft's husband, William Godwin, in his commentary on *A Vindication of the Rights of Woman*. As he comments: 'Many of the sentiments are undoubtedly of a rather masculine description. The spirited and decisive way in which the author explores the system of gallantry, and the species of homage with which the sex is usually treated, shocked the majority' (Godwin, cited in Taylor, 2005: 30).

However, as Taylor (2005: 30) comments, Wollstonecraft was far from being an uncritical spokesperson for 'a monolithic Enlightenment'. Wollstonecraft developed her thinking against the grain of mainstream enlightened opinion. Her book *A Vindication of the Rights of Woman* draws on Enlightenment perspectives to offer a scathing critique. As Taylor (2005: 30) notes: 'she mounted a systematic assault on "modern" writings on women which, in her view, portrayed women "as a kind of subordinate being, and not as a part of the human species" (Wollstonecraft, 1792)'.

Despite her critique, Wollstonecraft paid due deference to the key male philosophers of the Enlightenment as she laid out in her two *Vindications*, including Bacon, Locke, Adam Smith, Voltaire, Leibniz, Hume, Kant, Joseph Priestly and Rousseau, whose influence permeated thinking from 1788 onwards. Taylor argues that her *Historical and Moral View of the French Revolution* (1794), which was written in France at the height of the Terror and 'clandestinely slipped to her London publisher chapter-by-chapter interwove a detailed chronicle of the early stages of the revolution with a triumphalist account of the Enlightenment's advance across Europe and America' (Taylor, 2005: 31).

By the mid-1790s, Wollstonecraft was the most widely read political woman in Europe. However, as Peltz (2008: 112) shows: 'Wollstonecraft's posthumous reputation was badly served by Godwin's publication of her passionate and often anguished love-letters and the unfinished *Maria*, which excuses adultery, argues for women to have control over their own property and is frank about female sexual appetites'. *The European Magazine* called her 'a philosophical wanton'.

The critique of radical thinkers such as Wollstonecraft and Macaulay was powerful and was encapsulated in the Reverend Richard Polwhele's *The Unsex'd Females* (1798), which was a long verse diatribe and critique of late 18th-century feminist writers. As Peltz (2008: 113) comments: 'Using ... the category "unsex'd," Polwhele identified and attacked women who had abandoned "natural" modesty and deference, who supported the democratic politics of the French Revolution and who even went as far as to demand equality with men.'

Polwhele's criticism went beyond Wollstonecraft. Other women who were identified included the following published authors: Mary Hays, Helen Maria Williams, Catherine Macaulay, Anna Letitia Barbauld, Anne Jebb, Charlotte Smith, Mary Robinson and Anna Yearsley. Separately, Polwhele provides a list of women writers largely drawn from the bluestockings, including Elizabeth Montagu, Elizabeth

Carter, Fanny Burney, Hannah More and Anna Seward. His argument was that these earlier writers 'had cultivated female respectability and worked to build social ties between people rather than engineer political factions' (Peltz, 2008: 115).

Catherine Macaulay: 'female virago'

Catherine Macaulay was regarded as one of the leading political theorists and activists of her time. Her most significant work was the publication of her eight-volume study of the *History of England* (1763–83). The work was not a feminist critique but a radical republican analysis advocating political reform. As Peltz (2008: 96) writes: 'Macaulay's *History* focuses on key seventeenth century events – the Civil War, the execution of Charles I, and the impact of the Commonwealth – and was a highly charged contribution to the radical Whig programme for political reform.'

As was shown in Chapter Three, Macaulay's reach was more international than Wollstonecraft's, and her work was recognized in North America. Frazer (2011) argues that Macaulay's work was a direct influence on Wollstonecraft, and Hill (1995) shows that they did communicate, even though they never met (see Chapter Three).

Hill (1992: 132) shows many women wrote anonymously or under pseudonyms to 'protect themselves from male prejudice'. Macaulay published in this way, particularly for her polemical pamphlets. Her *History* was published under her own name, but, as Hill (1992: 132) comments, when 'the first volume was reviewed by *Gentleman's Magazine* it referred to its author as "Mrs Macaulay, Dr Macaulay's wife" (*Gentleman's Magazine*, 1766, 36: 439)'. The parochialism of Britain and its intellectual and political elite was not found in America. Benjamin Franklin was an admirer of Macaulay's *History* and he purchased the eight-volume work to include in the University of Virginia Library.

As noted in Chapter Three, despite being regarded as having much in common in philosophical terms, and having their work reviewed in the same journals, Macaulay and Wollstonecraft did never met, although there was limited communication between them. Frazer (2011: 604) comments that the December 1790 issue of the *Analytical Review* included reviews of both Wollstonecraft's *Vindication* and Macaulay's *Observations on the Reflections of … Edmund Burke on the Revolution in France*. Frazer notes that in November 1790 the *Analytical Review* had published an admiring review by Wollstonecraft of Macaulay's *Letters on Education* (1790).

Women writers of the 19th century

The 19th century saw the proliferation of women writers in the US. A range of women writers contributed to lifting the profile of women in the public sphere. The following are just a selection of women writers in the US during this time.

Hannah Adams (1755–1831) is known as the first professional woman writer in the US and was a distant cousin of John Adams. She wrote both theoretical works and histories, including *Summary History of New England* (1799), which was the first history to trace the genesis of the US from the *Mayflower* to the ratification of the Constitution.

Frances Hodgson Burnett (1849–1924) moved from Britain to the US when she was aged 16 and supported herself by writing for American magazines. She also gained success with the books she wrote for children, including *The Secret Garden, Little Lord Fauntleroy* and *A Little Princess*.

Kate Chopin (1851–1904) was born in Missouri and lived in Louisiana. She began to write to support herself and her children. She wrote *Bayou Folk* (1894), a collection of stories about life in Louisiana, which gave her national recognition. However, she is best known for the publication of her critically acclaimed novel *The Awakening* (1898), which deals with female independence through a suicidal female heroine who leaves her husband and children in an attempt to discover her personal freedom.

Sarah Josepha Buell Hale (1788–1879) was editor of the popular *Ladies' Magazine*. She gained widespread influence with American women from 1828 to 1877. Like many other women writers, she began writing after her husband died. In Hale's case, she was left pregnant and with four other children to care for. The women writers she published in her periodical helped to promote the idea of women as professional writers. The *Magazine* included correspondence, stories, poetry, music and fashion. Hale preferred to depict women in simple dress, as opposed to other magazines. Her fashion sense, which was focused on a more physically active life-style, lacked popular appeal and she chose to discontinue fashion features. She took up a number of national causes.

Gail Hamilton (1836–96) was an essayist, journalist and fiction writer who lived in Hamilton, Massachusetts, and was a school teacher and governess in Washington, DC. In the 1850s she started publishing for the anti-slavery paper *The National Era*, and went on to publish books on women's rights, politics, religion and children's subjects. She also sued her publisher, Ticknor and Fields, for underpayment and thus made a significant contribution to the position of professional women writers. Her books included: *Woman's Wrongs: A Counter-Irritant* (1868) and *Woman's Worth and Worthlessness* (1872).

Harriet Beecher Stowe (1811–96) is best known for her anti-slavery novel *Uncle Tom's Cabin* (1852), but she also wrote nine other novels, short fiction and non-fiction. She also wrote books based on her travels in Europe.

Whereas American women writers published on a variety of topics and in a variety of different forms, in Britain the novel tended to be the main form and focus for women writers. As Eger (2008: 134) notes, for writers such as Virginia Woolf and her 19th-century predecessors, 'the novel which was the genre traditionally associated with feminine authors, provided an important intellectual outlet ... The novel provided an important cultural space in which the role of women in society can be explored and developed.' Eger makes an important point in showing the succession through the novel between the bluestockings and 19th-century writers. 'It allowed women to investigate important questions of female cultural tradition and legacy that the bluestockings first established as integral to their identity as professional writers and artists' (Eger, 2008: 134).

Other women writers experimented with the novel form, including Jane Austen, who produced a satire of the Gothic novel in *Northanger Abbey*:

> 'And what are you reading, Miss –?' 'Oh! It is only a novel!' replies the young lady, while she lays down her book with affected indifference, or momentary shame. 'It is only *Cecilia* or *Camilla*, or *Belinda*'; or, in short, only some work in which the most thorough knowledge of human nature, the happiest delineation of its varieties, the liveliest effusions of wit and humour, are conveyed to the world in the best chosen language. (Austen, 2003: 24, cited in Eger, 2008: 136)

Eger (2008: 135) shows in this extract that 'Austen refers to her female contemporaries Fanny Burney (author of *Cecilia* and *Camilla*) and Maria Edgeworth (author of *Belinda*), in a defence of the novel as a moral genre that engages with human nature.'

The 20th-century novelist Jean Rhys was also influenced by Jane Austen, and wrote a prequel to *Jane Eyre* entitled *Wide Sargasso Sea* (1996), in which she described 'the painful story of the first Mrs Rochester connecting Bronte's female oppression with an analysis of racial oppression in the nineteenth century British Empire' (Eger, 2008: 136).

Despite the use of the novel by different women writers, there was no unanimity among them as writers. For example, Eger (2008: 139) shows that George Eliot was very critical of Wollstonecraft, whom she described as a 'ponderous intellectual' and that Eliot saw the *Vindication of the Rights of Woman* as 'eminently serious, severely moral and withal rather heavy' (Eliot, 1855: 201, cited in Eger).

Bloomsbury and beyond

The work of these novelists overlapped with and paved the way for the emergence of the Bloomsbury Group, including significant women writers and public intellectuals Virginia Woolf and Vanessa Bell. Woolf viewed women's economic independence as essential to women's freedom. Although the exact significance of the Bloomsbury Group is beyond the scope of this book, it is important to flag the intersection of literature and politics in their work. Marcus (2000), in her analysis of 'Woolf's Feminism and Feminism's Woolf', shows how Woolf's work is seen as one of the most effective examples of a literary feminist politics and, in addition, of establishing a specifically female literary tradition and women's language. Marcus (2000: 210) also shows how Woolf's work establishes a place for 'feminist anger or radicalism'; for the 'feminist use of "androgyny" as a concept'; for the 'relationship of socialism to feminism', 'feminism to pacifism' and 'patriarchy and fascism'.

Marcus (2000: 210) also shows how 'feminist criticism has brought about a major shift from accounts of Woolf's relationship with "Bloomsbury" men (Lytton Strachey, Roger Fry, Clive Bell) and their influence upon her to a concern with Woolf's relationship, personal, sexual and professional with other women (Vanessa Bell, Violet Dickenson, Vita Sackville-West, Ethel Smythe)'. Politically, Woolf was involved with suffrage work, including her work with the People's Suffrage Organization, which has been described as influential in historical and personal terms.

Woolf's two key feminist books were *A Room of One's Own* and *Three Guineas* – this in addition to her essays on women's position in society and other women writers. Marcus (2000: 217) points out that, as with many later and contemporary writers, it is difficult to draw strict lines between Woolf's feminist polemical works and her fiction; she notes that Woolf's 'methodology' in terms of feminist politics was both original and imaginative.

Conclusion

Regardless of the success of these women writers, and probably as a result of it, at the start of the 19th century the combined social and intellectual prominence of so many talented and scholarly women was responded to with both resentment and disgust by many men. An example of how men patronised and demeaned women is shown in the lithograph by the Irish painter Daniel Maclise entitled *Regina's Maid of Honour*, where he domesticates intellectual women in order to make them more palatable, while at the same time belittling their achievements. As Eger (2008: 132) writes:

> His subjects are ...: Anna Maria Hall (1800–81), Irish novelist and children's writer; Letitia Elizabeth Landon (1802–38), known as L.E.L, the best-selling and innovative poet; Lady Sydney Morgan (1783–1859), novelist and Irish nationalist, author of the famous *Wild Irish Girl* (1806); Harriet Martineau (1802–6), essayist, popular educator and political economist; Jane Porter (1776–1850), whose novel about Scottish independence ... was highly popular ...; Caroline Norton (1808–77), poet, novelist and pamphleteer; and finally, ... Marguerite, Countess of Blessington (1789–1849), novelist, journalist and literary hostess.

The growth of a range of social movements and the emergence of women as political activists across the social classes fundamentally moved the narrative forward as far as women, politics and the public sphere was concerned. These movements are developed in Chapter Five.

FIVE

The role of social movements leading to the emergence of women public intellectuals

The *fin de siècle* figure of the 'New Woman' may have been a journalistic construction, but contemporary commentators immediately recognised her in the women graduates from the new redbrick universities and women's colleges. An article in the students' magazine of Owens College, Manchester (where women were admitted from 1888) described her: 'She smokes. She rides a bicycle – not in skirts. She demands a vote. She belongs to a club. She would like a latch key – if she had not already got one. She holds drawing room meetings and draws crowds to public halls to discuss her place in the world.' (Cowman, 2010: 63)

Introduction

The idea of women public intellectuals is not a new concept and women have occupied positions in the public sphere historically. However, one of the clearest patterns of development that has led to the emergence of women public intellectuals has been the role of social movements that have propelled women's voices more fully into the public sphere. They have also articulated the role of women public intellectuals more fully. The bluestockings who have been discussed in earlier chapters were not a social movement per se – they were more a collection of learned, aristocratic individuals, despite their significant contribution to women's scholarship. Even the more radical writers and thinkers who were outside the bluestocking circles, Mary Wollstonecraft and Catherine Macaulay, did not really advocate directly for all women as independent thinkers and as worthy of the franchise. Social movements such as the suffrage movement and later feminist and civil rights movements were important in accelerating a more diverse and broad-based range of women into roles as public intellectuals. This chapter reviews the significance of social movements in accelerating women into the public sphere as public intellectuals.

The pre-social movement phase

In her analysis of women in British politics, Cowman (2010) argues that the emphasis of historians such as Amanda Vickery (2001) and others has given historical weight to suffrage as being the 'heroic voice' in the history of women's politics. However, as Cowman (2010: 2) indicates, this tends to imply that there is no history of women and politics prior to suffrage. Cowman goes on to show that this is an incorrect assessment.

Women were involved in politics from the 17th century onwards. Smith (1998) argues that women of a certain class were expected to participate in the political obligations of their family and that this informed the activities of aristocratic women in 17th-century royal courts. In addition, Smith (1998) shows, upper-class women in the 18th century took part in electoral politics on behalf of their husbands, fathers, brothers and were involved politically in their own right through networking opportunities for ambitious party men. Smith also points to the importance of 'the local' for women's politics for a variety of reasons, including those that are seen as non-political and feminine, such as education, childcare, caring for the sick and elderly and looking after the home.

In addition, women also took part in politics at all levels of society. For example, working-class women joined with men to express concerns over areas such as religious, economic and social matters in both popular demonstrations and riots in the 17th and 18th centuries. While these can be classed as generic social movements, they did not directly impact on women's position in politics.

Women, politics and print culture

Women were actively involved in the development of print culture from the mid–17th century onwards. They were involved in all aspects of the print industry as well as in authoring pamphlets and disseminating their ideas to a broader reading public. Crawford and Gowing (2000) maintain that a small number of women used print to challenge sexual inequality in ways that one can label feminist. However, as Cowman notes, this did not constitute collective social movements at this point.

Caine (1997) shows that at the end of the 18th century the French Revolution brought fresh impetus to debates concerning political rights. At the same time as this universalizing 'Rights of Man' came the first calls for women's political emancipation, which Caine (1997:

11) claims as 'marking the birth of modern feminism'. Hughes (1995) claims that petitioning by early modern women was seen as 'normal in many accounts, irritating or embarrassing perhaps, but a part of political life' (Hughes, 1995: 181, 175).

Mistresses and courtiers: aristocratic women and politics

A 'safer' role for women, Cowman states, was that of the courtier, which was a defined job with a salary, and this could be substantial. Sarah Churchill derived an annual income of around £6,000 from her various official positions as 'mistress of the robes', 'groom of the stole', 'keeper of the Privy Purse' and 'ranger of Windsor Park'. 'Sarah Churchill was one of the most frequently cited female canvassers, who embraced the more robust areas of electioneering when she headed to St Albans in 1705 to thwart the ambitions of the Tory, John Gape (*Commons Journals*, xv, 38)' (Cowman, 2010: 22). Cowman comments that towards the end of the 18th century, Georgiana, Duchess of Devonshire, was similarly censured for moving too frequently and freely among lower-class voters on behalf of the Whig campaign in 1784, leading to the accusations of a 'kiss for votes' scandal.

Amanda Vickery (2001), in *Women, Power and Privilege and its Impact on Politics in the Late Eighteenth and Early Nineteenth Century*, focuses on the political experiences of privileged women in Britain. Vickery and others note that they were in the strongest position to test the limits of women's political involvement, and that 'patrician women' enjoyed political clout because of their rank, family and property, so heiresses and female heads of families simply inherited power. Colley (1992) estimates that there were 21 different constituencies between 1790–1820 in which women exercised control.

Vickery notes that the Duchess of Devonshire was a well-known figure in terms of campaigning, and she indicates that it was the men in the family who encouraged her to take part in the Westminster election of 1784. The duchess's involvement was met with what Vickery calls 'salacious opprobrium' for her highly publicized canvassing of male voters in the Westminster constituency in support of Charles James Fox. Lewis (2001) maintains that there was an assumption that her activities were extraordinary and outrageous, and that the furore resulted in new boundaries on autonomous female action in public. However, as Lewis emphasizes: 'at the very moment Georgiana and her sister were canvassing the streets of Westminster, their mother, Lady Spencer, was managing the Spencer electoral interest in St Albans ...'. As Vickery

(2001: 11) comments, it is not the duchess's canvassing which needs to be explained, but the opposition to it.

The public castigation of the Duchess of Devonshire can be attributed to two factors, according to Foreman (1997): firstly, her direct style and autonomy apparently 'breached contemporary notions of femininity', while secondly, 'in forgetting her rank with male electors over ale and gin' she was seen 'committing "lèse-majesté" and thereby threatening hierarchy' (Vickery, 2001: 12). Foreman also notes that while the social and political response forced the duchess to display more 'self-conscious propriety', she remained at the forefront of Whig political life until her death in 1805.

Reynolds (1998) makes an important point that this kind of political activism was not about feminism. These women defined themselves as 'aristocratic' first and foremost and did not act with the interests of women at heart. Their view was summed up by Reynolds (1998: 1–2) in that their primary interest was in power for the aristocracy. However, Reynolds does acknowledge that despite the fact that peeresses were not summoned to take a seat in the House of Lords until 1958, gender remained an important factor for the aristocracy as regards power.

Mandler (2001) goes further in his analysis of the relationship between aristocratic women and power by arguing that a powerful 'masculinised culture of political virtue' that drew on republican Rome 'influenced the governing families severely curtailing male tolerance of female assertiveness'. The Duchess of Devonshire's behaviour and noble rank meant that she was removed from most ordinary people and women and, as Vickery states, she was not seen as a role model – although possibly as an icon. As Vickery notes, the duchess and her squadrons made princely purchases during the 1784 election.

Print culture and politics

The 17th and 18th centuries saw an enormous expansion of print culture, and the vibrant print culture of the 17th century was followed by a growth in newspaper and political titles in the 18th century. Schwoerer (1998: 57) shows that there was a great expansion in the range of titles, with 700 new ones being published between 1620 and 1700.

Cowman (2010: 23) shows that 'the spread of print culture had other implications for women's politics. It reflected a growing level of women's literacy. More immediately print culture aided the evolution of certain spaces where pamphlets, newspapers and periodicals could be read and ideas discussed. A significant development was the popularity of the coffee-house, the first of which was opened in Oxford in 1650' (see Klein, 1996: 31).

Another important dimension for the emergence of women public intellectuals was the expansion of the intellectual environment for women. This was particularly the case in cities such as London. In London, women took part in debating societies, which proved to be a key site for the formation and spread of Enlightenment thought. As Cowman (2010: 24) writes, 'They became popular from the 1750s, first as male only groups, then ... opening to women. In 1780 *La Belle Assemblée*, the first female debating society, was launched ... Debating societies provided women with a public space where they could articulate their own analysis of varying aspects of their subordination.'

Women's political role in the French Revolution

Mary Wollstonecraft's (1792) *A Vindication of the Rights of Woman* is the most well-known articulation of women's rights in the context of debates around rights and the French Revolution. Cowman (2010: 25) argues that, as such, it is one of the founding texts of British feminism. However, its emphasis was a critique of the gendered nature of Enlightenment thought, as opposed to advocating the extension of specific civil and political rights for women. 'Yet in its own time, it represented one of the earliest attempts to critique the gendered nature of Enlightenment thought which universalised virtue on the one hand while questioning women's embodiment on the other hand' (Cowman, 2010: 25; and see Taylor, 1993).

Public and private spheres and the politics of gender

As has been shown earlier, the relationship between the emergence of women as public intellectuals and debates around the public and private spheres has relied on the work of Jürgen Habermas (1989). For Habermas it was the growth of a range of sites where public debate could take place, including the debating society, the assembly room, the subscription library and the coffee-house, combined with the expansion of the print media that represented the emergence of the bourgeois public sphere. The growth of print culture, as Habermas maintained, led to the emergence of public opinion. As Cowman (2010: 27) notes, the descriptions of the public and private spheres ascribed gender qualities to both.

A range of exclusionary practices supported the gendered division, which had the effect of marginalizing women from the public sphere as the institutions became more formalized. Davidoff and Hall (1987) outlined the restrictions and closure for women and showed how these shaped 19th-century middle-class identity. However, Vickery challenged this view and argued against the idea of a 'golden age' for women that characterized an earlier period. As Morgan (2007: 4) comments, 'rather than beating on the doors of the ancient fortress, women were very much part of the process of constructing a public sphere in the city'.

Women and organized political action before suffrage

Women were actively involved in the anti-slavery movement, which, as Cowman notes, bridged two centuries but gained national cohesion as a movement after 1800. As Cowman (2010: 33) observes, 'Eighteenth century women showed their support in a number of ways. They donated substantially, around a quarter of the published income of the Manchester abolition society came from subscribers in 1788' (see Midgley, 2007). Cowman (2010: 33) outlines some of the activities:

> They made public display of their opposition, wearing Wedgwood cameos featuring a kneeling slave above the words 'am I not a man and brother' as brooches and hairpins and bracelets that made fashion into a political statement. They were enthusiastic supporters of William Fox's abstention campaign, which urged the public to employ their economic power to undermine enterprises which relied on slavery ... Abstention anticipated the exclusive dealing of Chartist women by some 40 years, and has been associated with a broader more radical challenge to anti-slavery's London leadership through its connection to the demand for immediate emancipation regardless of parliamentary schedules.

Women campaigned door-to-door to build support and also established public meetings. However, Midgley shows that they remained part of the rank and file and were not asked to speak on public platforms. However, women were prepared to stand up to the male leadership. Midgley shows how, in the late 1830s, Mary Anne Rawson, from Sheffield, led a revolt against the men's society over what men regarded as their compromising attitude to calling for immediate emancipation for West Indian apprentices.

Cowman provides an interesting analysis of the intersection of class and gender in the anti-slavery movement. She shows how divisions between women emerged in relation to the anti-slavery movement based on class. Women's anti-slavery activism came from middle-class membership and some working-class support. However, poorer women pointed out the unfairness of wealthier women encouraging them to buy more expensive 'free grown' sugar, oblivious to the economic implications for poorer households. Cowman (2010: 34) highlights the differences in perspective of different women:

> Some women such as Elizabeth Heyrick argued for an egalitarian perspective which encouraged her to demand a more active and equal role in the campaign. Others such as Hannah More believed in spiritual equality regardless of gender or race, but retained a commitment to a hierarchical social order and did not wish their campaign to lead to women being given a broader political role.

Later 'bluestocking' groups: the Langham Place circle and the Kensington Society

Jane Rendall's (1985) *The Origin of Modern Feminism* sees the origins of modern feminism in the mid-19th century and identifies the anti-slavery movement as critical for the emergence of a more organized women's movement. However, the emphasis was not on improvements in the position of women. But this changed in the mid-19th century, when women began to demand greater rights.

Cowman claims that the most influential grouping was an informal network of women named 19 Langham Place, which was the office of the early 'feminist paper' the *English Woman's Journal*. The *Journal* was founded by Barbara (Leigh Smith) Bodichon and her friend Bessie Rayner Parkes in 1858 to offer a wider platform for discussion of women's work and concerns. They wanted the *Journal* to be a campaigning tool as well as a periodical. Parkes wanted to set up a bookshop and club around it. A network of women active in various campaigns developed around this, including Emily Davies, Adelaide Proctor, Matilda Hays and Emily Faithful. The *Journal* expanded in 1859 when a friend of Matilda Hays, Theodosia Monson, took more spacious premises at Langham Place for the *Journal*. This included a coffee-shop and a reading room that could be used for other activities.

The *Journal* itself was a departure from earlier publications and provided employment opportunities for women and started a register of women seeking work for circulation among subscribers. Because of the overwhelming demand from women for positions, Jessie Boucherett took charge of the register and established the Society for Promoting the Employment of Women (SPEW). Cowman shows that Boucherett identified the lack of training as a key obstacle to women gaining employment. As a result, SPEW started classes in bookkeeping and literacy and worked with employers to place its students. In addition, Cowman reports that another activist, Emily Faithful, set up a printing firm, the Victoria Printing Press, which trained and employed a small number of women compositors. The press gained a royal warrant and printed the *English Woman's Journal*. As Cowman (2010: 42) comments, 'The *Journal* carried a range of articles discussing the sort of labour that women might be able to undertake, as well as arguing for better educational provision to enhance women's employability.'

The women activists of Langham Place also campaigned for the expansion of opportunities in higher education and educational provision for girls. Cowman (2010: 42) notes that a small number of institutions were opened, including the North London Collegiate School (1850) and Cheltenham's Ladies College (1854). In addition, through Emily Davies and with the financial support of Barbara Bodichon, they set up Girton College in Cambridge. With the expansion of women's educational opportunities 'they also called for greater access to the professions, backing Elizabeth Garrett as she struggled to qualify as a doctor' (Cowman, 2010: 42). Disappointingly, the *English Woman's Journal* was not a financial success and was wound up in 1864.

There were also disagreements among women activists at Langham Place over the focus and direction of the movement. As Cowman (2010: 42) notes, 'Parkes became increasingly cautious, criticising married women's work outside the home and wanting to avoid contentious issues such as women's suffrage or sexuality.' As a result, a new group was formed, known as the Kensington Debating Society. The object of this group was to 'serve as a sort of link between persons, above the average of thoughtfulness and intelligence who are interested in common subjects, but who have not many opportunities of mutual intercourse (see Dingsdale, 1856–66)' (Cowman, 2010: 42).

Cowman points out that both these groups were significant in that they represented a development in the way women organized themselves. Women, through groups such as these, were beginning to address issues that related to their social and legal status. This is shown by Rendall (1985), who claims that they began to define a 'cautious, liberal-feminist politics' that set the tone for the emergence of the early women's movement.

Development of issue-based politics in the women and politics agenda

One of the key issues for married women was married women's property rights, and Barbara Bodichon was particularly active in this regard. In 1854 she published a pamphlet, *A Brief Summary of the Laws of England Concerning Women, Together with a Few Observations Thereon*. She organized a petition that attracted 26,000 signatures, including those of the poet Elizabeth Barrett Browning, George Eliot and Mrs Gaskell. While the petition failed, some of the demands were incorporated into the 1857 Divorce Act, which linked areas of reform on the legal foundations of marriage and broader feminist critiques of the legal aspects of marriage.

Other political inroads into the legal framework of married women's property rights were included by the Liberal government of 1880, and the Married Women's Property Acts of 1881 (Scotland) and 1882 (England) increased women's independence. While the English Act did not end coverture (the legal premise that a wife was subordinate to her husband), it weakened it significantly by allowing married women to act as independent legal entities.

Broadening the role of women as public intellectuals

One of the ways that women broadened the scope of their public visibility and engagement was through philanthropic vocations. This work developed a strong political dimension as local government began to take over the work of voluntary societies. As Cowman (2010: 48) indicates, the growth of philanthropic organizations in the 19th century led to their professionalization. This led to greater national recognition for women and, indeed, their empowerment. Mica Nava (1996: 44) shows how philanthropy established women's position in the public sphere more fully:

> It authorised the observation and classification of the homes, lives and even marital relationships of the poor. Middle-class women involved in the philanthropic enterprise were not obliged to conduct their affairs with a lowered gaze. They could indulge their pleasures of urban spectatorship – of the voyeur – with a sense of entitlement.

Cowman maintains that many historians see women's philanthropic work as a step towards greater involvement in local government at the end of the 19th century. Hollis (1987), in a study of women in local government, came to the conclusion that this did little to increase the case of parliamentary suffrage for women.

Cowman (2010: 55) also shows that the structural landscape of politics was changing, although she shows that there is no agreement on the date when this changed. She notes that

> by the mid-nineteenth century a form of modern party system was emerging. However at that point, no political party recognised women as members (this would not change until the birth of the independent Labour Party in 1892). Women increasingly developed a foothold in political parties and were able to work in both political parties and in the women's movement.

Changes to the political landscape: women, politics and social movements

The suffrage movement can be traced to 1897 and the establishment of the National Union of Women's Suffrage Societies (NUWSS), which was set up under the leadership of Millicent Garrett Fawcett. The object of the movement was to campaign to secure votes for women on the same terms that they were offered to men.

Women and suffrage

A new suffrage society was established in Manchester in 1903, the Women's Social and Political Union (WSPU), which was inaugurated by Emmeline Pankhurst. As Cowman (2010: 64) shows, the Pankhursts were early members of the Independent Labour Party in Manchester, and Emmeline Pankhurst was the first woman elected to the National Executive Committee. Cowman also indicates that she was a committed suffragist and was impatient with the Labour Party's lack of activity on the issue of suffrage.

The WSPU recruited younger women who were fearless and unafraid to confront hostile crowds. Cowman (2010: 63) comments on the emergence of this 'New Woman': see the opening quote in this chapter on page 67.

Lawrence (2001), in 'Contesting the Male Polity: the Suffragettes and the Politics of Disruption in Edwardian Britain', notes that during the period of partial male democracy between 1867 and 1914, notions of 'manliness' and male 'honour' were in the ascendancy, and he notes that force was central in the political meeting. Lawrence maintains that the undercurrent of violence at political meetings made them overwhelmingly male environments and women rarely spoke at formal political meetings.

Lawrence makes the point that women's involvement in party politics did not start with the suffragettes' campaign of militancy in the mid-1900s, but that there was a long tradition of women's involvement in both 'high' and 'low' forms of political activity. He (Lawrence, 2001: 204) observes that '"plebeian women" could also claim a long and honourable tradition of involvement in public politics and that women were active participants in food riots in the eighteenth century'. Lawrence also shows that women were subjected to violence by party members and members of the audience at political events. Elizabeth Robins in *The Convert* (1907 [1980]) shows that the violence was often overtly sexual.

Beyond suffrage: feminist organizations 1920–79

While suffrage issues dominated the women's movement for half a century, it would be entirely mistaken to see the movement as limited to the vote. As Cowman (2010: 150) shows, 'the failure of the Women's Party experiment in 1918 undermined attempts at a "feminisation of politics" via an autonomous sex-based party'.

Historians have generally argued that there was 'a lull' in feminist politics in the inter-war period. Over the period of the 1940s and 1950s, Catherine Blackford identifies 10 different groupings that can be identified as feminist, including: 'the Association for Social and Moral Hygiene, the London and National Society (later the Fawcett Society), the Married Women's Association, the Open Door Council, the St John's Social and Political Alliance, the Six Point Group, the Status of Women Committee, the Suffragettes Fellowship, Women for Westminster and the Women's Freedom League'. Cowman also identifies other groupings including the National Union of Societies for Equal Citizenship (NUSEC) and the Women's Publicity and Planning Association, which she argues shows that gender-based politics was thriving in extra-parliamentary organizations even though parliamentary politics remained dominated by party concerns that excluded a gender focus.

Feminism and the women's liberation movement (WLM) has been the subject of significant commentary and debate by a wide range of writers. It is beyond the scope of this book to pursue a chronology and analysis of the emergence of the WLM and feminism more generally. Brooks (1997) has a detailed analysis of the growth of feminism and the WLM, and the multitude of its divisions highlights the difficulties of the coherence of an inter-generational feminist movement.

The complexity of the emergence of feminism and the WLM highlighted the historical importance of early activists and suffragettes. Cowman (2010: 165) notes that 'the first National Women's Liberation Movement Conference was held at Ruskin College Oxford in February 1970 and attracted 600 delegates'. Cowman indicates that the conference became an annual event, growing to 3,000 delegates in 1977, until its final meeting in 1978.

Different branches of feminism and the WLM produced some significant women public intellectuals, including Valerie Amos. Amos was particularly prominent in the emergence of black feminism and in its critique of WLM as marginalizing the position of black women (see Amos and Parmar, 1984). Radical feminism saw the growth of the issues of rape, sexuality and violence as major issues and the growth, indirectly, of the Women's Aid Federation, which started in Chiswick in 1972.

Cowman also notes, perhaps significantly, that many women moved from the WLM into party politics or academia, particularly on the Left, where they began to demand greater representation in political structures.

Conclusion

The role of social movements was important in defining women public intellectuals politically. The growth of social movements has to be set alongside the expansion of higher education for women, as well as the expansion of the print industry. This led to an expansion and broadening of the base of women's participation in political activity, particularly around specific campaigns and causes. Women were actively involved, individually and collectively, in a number of campaigns prior to the emergence of the suffrage movement. The intersection of gender and class was an important factor leading to the growth of both political activism and, more specifically, the emergence of the suffragettes and later WLM. Analysis shows that the motivation of most women was pragmatic and issue based as opposed to ideological. Issue-based politics covered all social classes and thus brought women together in social activism and within social movements.

SIX

Contemporary women public intellectuals: the United States (1)

Introduction

The last two chapters of the book analyse the contribution of a range of contemporary women public intellectuals who have moved from being highly successful academics in universities in the US into roles in different political administrations of the US, both Republican and Democrat. While their position circumscribes their commentary as public intellectuals, they have established themselves as significant women contributors to social and political discourse. In each case they are analysed in relation to early years, their academic career, their noteworthy publications, their service to the administration and their contribution and legacy as public intellectuals. Chapter Six provides an analysis of three high-profile women public intellectuals: Condoleezza Rice, Samantha Power and Susan Rice.

Female leadership in higher education

An article on female leadership in the world's top universities, in *The Times Higher Education* (*THE*) on 8 March 2018 maintains that female leadership in the world's top universities is actually moving backwards. Bothwell (2018) shows that the number of top universities led by women has declined in the last year, which is in contrast to the recent progress made in closing the gender gap. This is according to *THE* world rankings data.

Bothwell reports that just 34, or 17%, of the top 200 universities in the latest 2018 rankings have a female leader, two fewer than in 2017. The country with the highest proportion of female university leaders is Sweden, and Bothwell shows that of the six Swedish institutions that make it into the top 200, four are led by women. Additionally, Bothwell shows that one of Spain's two universities represented in the top 200 is female led – the Autonomous University of Barcelona – and two of Switzerland's seven representative universities have a female leader.

As one might expect, the US has the highest number of female presidents, at 11, accounting for 32% of female leaders in the top 200. Seven of the 34 female leaders in the top 200, or 21%, are leaders of UK universities, including Louise Richardson, vice-chancellor of the world's highest-ranked university, the University of Oxford. Bothwell shows that while gender parity in the US is little better than the average for the entire top 200, with only 18% of elite American universities headed by a woman, UK universities are outperforming the global average with 23% of their top universities having a female leader. The figure was 19% per cent for both nations in the previous year, 2017.

Of the 27 countries that are in the top 20, 17 have no female university leaders. The top 10 universities led by women in 2018 include the University of Oxford (1), led by Louise Richardson; Harvard University (6), led by Drew Faust; Imperial College London (8), led by Alice Gast; University of Pennsylvania (10), led by Amy Guttman; University of California, Berkeley (19), led by Carol Christ; Cornell University (19), led by Martha Pollock; London School of Economics and Political Science (LSE) (25), led by Minouche Shafik; University of Washington (25), led by Ana Mari Cause; McGill University (42), led by Suzanne Fortier; and University of Wisconsin-Madison (43), led by Rebecca Blank. The analysis of 199 universities was based on university leaders in post on 1 March 2018.

Condoleezza Rice

> Uncowed by the prospect of failure, Rice has made a career of arriving in positions of power during difficult times and critics say, without the requisite experience. At 35, she advised President George W. Bush, who named her national security advisor in 2001; again she was the youngest person to ever hold the position. After eight years in Washington, Rice returned to Stanford as professor of political science and a senior fellow of the Hoover Institution. (Bell, 2010)

Jonathan Freedland, in an article in *The New York Times*, 1 July 2007, reviews Marcus Mabry's *Twice as Good*, which is a biographical analysis of Condoleezza Rice. Freedland makes the point that Rice has regularly enjoyed poll numbers 20 points higher than those of the men she serves. In 2006, Freedland notes, she topped an *Esquire* survey of women whom men would most like to take to a dinner party, ahead of Angelina Jolie, Julia Roberts, Oprah Winfrey and Jennifer

Aniston. Despite this, Freedland makes the point that the views of the colleagues she served with – Colin Powell, Donald Rumsfeld and Dick Cheney – are more well known.

Early years

Condoleezza Rice's speech to the Republican Party, 30 August 2012, as reported by Amy Davison Sorkin, reflects important aspects of her personal and political thinking:

> "My fellow Americans, ours has never been a narrative of grievance and entitlement. We never believed that I am doing poorly because you are doing well. We have never been jealous of one another and never envious of each other's success.
> "A little girl grows up in Jim Crow Birmingham. The segregated city of the South, where her parents cannot take her to a movie, theatre or to restaurants, but they have convinced her that even if she cannot have a hamburger at Woolworths, she can be the President of the United States if she wanted to be, and she becomes the Secretary of State."
> (Cited in Sorkin, 2012)

In these comments Rice offers a caricature of liberal positions – and a rejection of them. She is in effect saying that her parents were telling her to ignore the present and think of the future.

In his book *Twice as Good: Condoleezza Rice and Her Path to Power* (2007) Marcus Mabry provides a sympathetic biography of Condoleezza Rice and focuses on her formative years. Drezner (2008), in his review of Mabry's book, argues that 'Mabry's thesis is that Rice's strengths are also her weakness. Her focus, discipline, determined optimism and grace under pressure enabled her to overcome race and gender barriers (as well as former Secretary of Defense, Donald Rumsfeld). However, this also makes her unable to acknowledge failings, unable to acknowledge errors in judgement.'

However, Condoleezza Rice brought to the table a unique understanding of the socio-political context in which she grew up. As she shows in the following extracted section from her latest book, *Democracy: Stories from the Long Road to Freedom* (2017):

> As a child, I was part of another great awakening: the second founding of America, as the civil rights movement

unfolded in my hometown in Birmingham, Alabama, and finally expanded the meaning of 'We the people' to encompass people like me. There is nothing more thrilling than the moment when people finally seize their rights and their liberty.

Academic career

Rice's intellectual prowess has been the subject of significant criticism, given the elevated positions she has held in academia and in the Bush administration. Her academic career is a strong one. She earned her bachelor's degree in political science, cum laude, and Phi Beta Kappa from the University of Denver; her Master's from the University of Notre Dame; and her PhD from the Graduate School of International Studies at the University of Denver.

In a rather unpleasant assessment of Rice's scholarship, Brown (2008), in his article '10 Percent Intellectual: the Mind of Condoleezza Rice', maintains that at Notre Dame, where her academic papers were assessed by her adviser, George A. Brinkley, a Soviet scholar commented on her essays as follows:

> 'It lacked depth and attention to different interpretations and points of view ... her evident skills and potential were not developed into more mature scholarship'. At Notre Dame she received a 'terminal M.A.' (a degree not leading to a PhD). She then returned to the University of Denver where she wrote another M.A. thesis titled 'Music and Politics in the Soviet Union', 'not a fantastic piece', in terms of scholarship. She received her PhD in 1981, and published it in 1984 by Princeton University Press ... The book was mercilessly panned in the *American Historical Review* by Joseph Kalvoda. She published little and nothing of consequence. The article that helped her get tenure at Stanford is titled 'The Party, the Military and Decision Authority in the Soviet Union', *World Politics* in 1987.

As professor of political science, Rice had been on the Stanford faculty since 1981 and won two of the highest teaching honours – the 1984 Walter J. Gores Award for Excellence in Teaching and the 1993 School of Humanities and Sciences Dean's Award for Distinguished Teaching. She was a beneficiary of affirmative action programmes when hired as a political science professor at Stanford, but as provost she rejected that policy in making tenure decisions.

Rice served on President George H.W. Bush's National Security Council (NSC) staff. She served as Senior Director of Soviet and East European Affairs and Special Assistant to the President for National Security Affairs. In 1986 she also served as Special Assistant to the Director of the Joint Chiefs of Staff (see below).

In the US, being invited to serve in political administrations does not involve a resignation from an academic position and generally involves a leave of absence or secondment. Universities benefit from the reflected prestige and academics do not have to give up an academic career for political/administrative service. Such arrangements do not exist in the UK, thus limiting the academic calibre of government and limiting the experience of academics in academia. There is far more in the way of direct appointments to positions in the administrations in the US.

Rice returned to Stanford and served as Stanford University's provost from 1993 to 1999, during which time she was the institution's chief budget and academic officer. As provost, she was responsible for a $1.5 billion annual budget and the academic programme involving 1,400 faculty members and 14,000 students. In 1997 she also served on the Federal Advisory Committee on Gender-Integrated Training in the Military.

It might seem stunning to most academics that Rice should be appointed as provost with no management experience. In an interview with Katherine Bell in the *Harvard Business Review* (2010), Rice discusses her view in taking on the position:

> "Well I had one advantage. It was clear what my focus should be. Stanford was in deep economic trouble – we still had $157 million of earthquake damage – so I knew that budget stability and rebuilding the campus were my primary responsibilities. I had also just come out of Washington and I felt I'd been in pretty big shoes being the Soviet specialist at the end of the Cold War, and so I just sort of took it on. Early on I didn't know how to delegate. I was always trying to do other people's jobs. I learnt you'll drive yourself crazy doing that, and you won't have good people working for you very long. I got better at delegating, I think, after that."

The linkages between publication and policy development can be advantaged in this process. Rice wrote *Germany Unified and Europe*

Transformed (Zelikow and Rice, 1995) with Philip Zelikow, who is described as a lawyer, diplomat and historian. Brown (2008) comments that Zelikow drafted the original manuscript. Rice drew on Zelikow at a later point while serving in the George W. Bush administration in 2002.

From 2005 to 2009, Rice served as the 66th Secretary of State of the US, the second woman and the first African-American woman to hold the post. She also served as President George W. Bush's Assistant to the President for National Security Affairs (National Security Adviser) from 2001 to 2005, the first woman to hold the position.

After eight years in Washington, Rice returned to Stanford in 2009. She is currently the Denning Professor in Global Business and the Economy at the Stanford Graduate School of Business; the Thomas and Barbara Stephenson Senior Fellow on Public Policy at the Hoover Institution; and a professor of political science at Stanford University.

Some have encouraged Rice to stand for public office again, including for the presidency, against Trump. Charles Krauthammer, a conservative columnist but significant critic of Trump, was on *Fox News* on 11 May 2016, proposing Rice as the new FBI director after the public and undignified sacking of James Comey by Trump. Krauthammer suggested that Rice's background as a Russia specialist made her a good candidate for the new FBI director, who could oversee the investigation of the 2016 election hacking. From an interview with Susan Glasser (2017) in *Politico Magazine*, Rice, at least at present, seems to be settled into an academic role, as she admitted to Glasser: "Anything I can do from California I'm prepared to do. I'm a very happy professor" (Glasser, 2017).

Service in the administration

Rice was the first African-American woman to serve in significant higher-level positions in US administrations. She served as George W. Bush's Assistant to the President for National Security Affairs (National Security Adviser) from 2001 to 2005, being the first woman to hold the position; and, as stated, from 2005 to 2009, she served as the 66th Secretary of State of the US, the second woman to hold the post.

Drezner (2008), in his review of three contemporary books on Rice, makes a rather scathing comment on her performance in the role of National Security Adviser and Secretary of State. He comments: 'Among foreign policy cognoscenti, the consensus opinion is that Condoleezza Rice has been a below-average-to-disastrous national security adviser and an average secretary of state. She outlasted or outfoxed bureaucratic rivals to become George W. Bush's most trusted adviser in foreign affairs.'

In his overview of the three books on Rice – Marcus Mabry's (2007) *Twice as Good: Condoleezza Rice and her Path to Power*; Elizabeth Bumiller's (2007) *Condoleezza Rice: An America Life*; and Glen Kessler's (2007) *The Confidante: Condoleezza Rice and the Creation of the Bush Legacy* – Drezner provides an interesting account of their views. Drezner (2008) notes that Rice was

> a disciple of former National Security Adviser, Brent Scrowcroft's realist internationalism for most of her policy making career, she embraced much of the neo-conservative agenda following the September 11 attacks – and yet on becoming secretary of state, she jump-started multi-lateral diplomacy with the regimes of Pyongyang [North Korea] and Tehran [Iran].

Mabry's commentary on Rice is seen by Drezner as the most sympathetic and has been outlined above. Bumiller was White House correspondent from 2001 to 2006 and her coverage is focused on Rice's National Security Council tenure. She identifies most of the Bush administration's bigger foreign policy blunders as being the result of Rumsfeld's and Vice-President Dick Cheney's approach, which was to cut out Rice from decision making. Bumiller also indicates that there was implicit sexism in much of this. She also notes that Rice tolerated 'a dysfunctional interagency process' for far too long, despite evidence that all was not well.

Kessler's assessment of Rice's performance focuses on the first two years. He was the State Department's chief correspondent and argues that Rice found herself changing course on numerous issues – particularly on democracy promotion. Kessler also shows that Rice's alienation from the State Department's foreign service officers presents a parallel to her experience as Stanford provost.

Brown (2008) tends to confirm the assessment of Rice by Bumiller and Mabry, which suggests that in her '[a]scendance to power, Rice's main instrument has not been ground-breaking thinking about important intellectual issues, but rather what Mabry characterizes as "her phenomenal skill at spinning"'. Kaplan (2012) goes further and makes the following comment: 'To watch Condoleezza Rice, the face of George W. Bush's foreign policy, stand before a convention of cheering Republicans condemning Barack Obama for diminishing America's standing in the world – one can only gasp'. Kaplan goes on to say: 'Condi Rice – a top adviser in the most disastrous reputation-crippling foreign policy administration in decades – has no obvious business lecturing anybody on this score.'

It should not be assumed that Rice had no impact in terms of her contribution to the Bush administration. James Mann (2004), in his book *Rise of the Vulcans*, reports that

> when Richard Haas, a senior aide to Secretary of State Colin Powell and the director of policy planning at the State Department, drafted for the administration an overview of America's national security strategy following the September 11, 2001 attacks, Dr Rice, the national security advisor, 'ordered that the document be completely rewritten. She thought the Bush administration needed something bolder, something that would represent a more dramatic break with the ideas of the past. Rice turned the writing over to her old colleague, University of Virginia Professor Philip Zelikow'. The document, issued on September 17, 2002, is generally recognised as a significant document in the War on Terrorism.

Rice was quoted as stating to her students at Stanford: "Policy-making is 90 percent blocking and tackling and 10 percent intellectual."

Rice moved from National Security to the State Department, and in her interview with Bell (2010) had the following view: "I loved being in the White House. I was a few paces from the president, I saw him six, seven times a day. I admire[d] him, and loved working with him closely. But when you are not national security advisor, it's like trying to run foreign policy by remote control. So on balance I much preferred being secretary of state."

Publications: books and articles

Rice, as one would expect, has produced a number of books, several of which reflect on her personal experiences in relation to serving in the administration of George W. Bush and in relation to her family. Some of these include: *The Strategy of Campaigning* (Skinner et al, 2007); *Extraordinary Ordinary People: A Memoir of Family* (2010); and *No Higher Honor: A Memoir of My Years in Washington* (2011). She has also written a number of articles on foreign policy, published in *Foreign Affairs* (Rice: 2000, 2008). Possibly, the publication that has attracted the most interest is her latest book, *Democracy: Stories from the Long Road to Freedom* (2017). In his review of Rice's book in the *New York Times* in May 2017, Walter Russell Mead (2017) sets out a key quote from Rice which he sees as setting the tone for the book, as outlined earlier, where she talks of being part of the 'great awakening' encapsulated by the civil rights movement.

Mead says that Rice's point in *Democracy* is that this vision should shape the mission of American foreign policy in the 21st century. Mead comments that

> Rice's continuing defense of the democracy agenda will be much noted among Republicans seeking to come to terms with the implications of President Trump's 'America First' approach to the world. She is one of the country's most distinguished and widely respected diplomats. As hard-line advisers like Vice-President Dick Cheney and Secretary of Defense Donald Rumsfeld lost influence with President Bush in the years following the 2003 invasion of Iraq, Rice as secretary of state in the second Bush term emerged as the single most influential voice shaping foreign policy.

Mead notes that this framework was one that characterized the Clinton, Bush and Obama administrations but changed with the Trump administration.

In her interview with Susan B. Glasser in *Politico Magazine* in May 2017, Rice says that American democracy will survive Donald Trump. She acknowledges her concerns about a president accused of eroding democracy at home and ignoring it abroad.

In Mead's review of Rice's book, he points out that the results of the 2016 election make democracy promotion perhaps the most endangered element of the 'new world order' agenda. Mead sees *Democracy* as Rice's attempt to hammer home the idea of democracy promotion as a key goal for American foreign policy.

However, Rice is aware that mistakes made in the Bush administration have complicated the 'democracy project'. For example, the mistakes made in Iraq and the mistreatment of prisoners at Abu Ghraib, as well as 2016 elections which she and her team encouraged the Palestinians to engage but Hamas won.

Glasser (2017) argues that Rice's book *Democracy* has been greeted as a 'repudiation of Trump's America First worldview', as the *Washington Post* reported. Glasser notes that Rice called on Trump to withdraw from the 2016 election after the 'Access Hollywood' tape, and that she expressed alarm at the 'political wave of rising populism, nativism, protectionism and isolationism that helped boost Trump's election, calling them "the Four Horsemen of the Apocalypse'".

As Glasser says, Rice is a 'circumspect diplomat' when it comes to Trump. She has also recently visited him in the Oval Office to discuss China policy. Her recommendation of Rex Tillerson as Secretary of State has clearly been disastrous, both in Tillerson's disdain of Trump (calling Trump 'a moron') and in Trump's subsequent firing of Tillerson without ceremony.

Rice is surprisingly tolerant of Trump, possibly hoping to ward off the pressure of being considered as a possible challenger for the next election against Trump. As Glasser (2017) comments,

> She repeatedly says 'it's early days' when it comes to Trump's presidency, notes encouraging signs of foreign policy flip-flops such as Trump's missile strike in Syria to retaliate for an Assad regime chemical weapons attack on civilians and asserts her optimistic faith that 'American political institutions from the courts to the media will constrain Trump's authoritarian impulses'.

Glasser also notes that Rice's remarkably diplomatic approach to Trump is not surprising, given her reputation as a cautious 'inside player'. While Glasser notes that Rice is no fan of Trump, she is not prepared to launch or lead an opposition. As Glasser states, Rice falls back on 'the constraints' built into the system. As Rice comments: 'Democracy is built for disruption', she says. 'People are going to challenge the institutions, but the institutions I have absolute faith in, and whatever we're going through now, I have tremendous faith in them and that they're going to hold.'

Rice is scathing about Russia's hacking of the US election and encourages the Senate Intelligence Committee to act on this. She also advocates more forceful moves to counter Putin abroad, including arming the Ukrainians, which Trump does not support. She has a clear-headed understanding of Putin, which, in the light of the nerve agent poisoning in the UK, seems very accurate. Rice says of Putin that he is a 'kind of an eye-for-eye person', and she thinks he 'would have interfered because, in his view, we called his elections fraudulent in 2012, which they were. And now he's going to demonstrate that he can undermine our confidence in our elections.'

Concerns about democracy and democratic values are widespread among Republicans and Democrats in the Trump era. In her book, Rice considers a range of countries, including Russia,

Kenya, Columbia, Poland and Iraq and considers their democratic struggles.

As Lozada (2017), writing in *The Washington Post*, comments, Rice mixes 'realism and idealism'. She relies on 'institutional equilibrium' to retain 'democratic structures in the Trump era'. Interestingly, Lozada refers to the new epilogue to Rice's book after the 2017 presidential inauguration, where she refers to the 'new president' and is critical of politicians who scapegoat immigrants, stoke nationalism and criticize institutions. However, Rice's view is that the idea of democracy being threatened is 'alarmist and premature'.

Contribution and legacy as a public intellectual

While the contribution and legacy of Rice is a mixed one, no one can detract from her contribution and achievements as an African-American academic woman and public intellectual.

Freedland (2007) is critical of Rice, whom he sees as badly flawed. He argues that she presided over a dysfunctional security apparatus and was never able to bring the 'warring Defense and State Departments' together. Freedland also says that she ignored warnings about the 'Qaeda threat' and the risks of an Iraq invasion. Rice is most critical of her own failings in the role of National Security Adviser when she was unable to bring cohesion.

Wolfson (2008), in his commentary on Rice's legacy for CBS News, says that as America's top diplomat she did recognize changes in the world and did institute reforms in the Foreign Service and brought far more diplomats into posts in India, Pakistan, Brazil and Nigeria and fewer to more glamorous postings.

Rice also travelled more than her predecessors and visited more countries and met more with traditional allies. She was the first secretary of state to visit Libya for 50 years and particularly worked with moderate Arab states. However, Wolfson (2008) comments that 'An unnamed official said "ninety percent of events don't produce anything" … This may be a particularly harsh view but others asked to sum up Rice's tenure were not overly kind.'

Wolfson says that Rice can take credit for a number of policy successes, including the restoration of full diplomatic relations with Libya and progress in the Israeli–Palestinian conflict.

> After isolating North Korea in their first term and naming Pyongyang a member of the "axis of evil", Rice persuaded Bush to reverse course and engage in negotiations with

North Korea through the so-called Six Party Process. During two years of intense and often frustrating negotiations led by Ambassador Christopher Hill, North Korea, in return for economic benefits and being taken off Washington's state sponsor of terrorism list ... Rice said: "I think moving them from an American problem to something the international community agrees on how to solve is a very important step". (Wolfson, 2008)

Finally, Wolfson (2008) points out that possibly 'Condoleezza Rice's biggest asset as secretary of state was her close working relationship with her boss and that allowed her to make significant adjustments in some policies, most notably showing flexibility in dealing with North Korea. Rice was clearly a stronger advocate in internal foreign policy debates as secretary of state than she was as national security advisor.'

Samantha Power

I was expecting this sort of N.G.O. girl, considering her past, considering the book she wrote. Actually she is a nice mixture of liberal interventionism and realpolitik. (Gerard Araud, French Ambassador to Washington, previously at the UN, cited in Osmos, 2014)

There's been more than one time when I find out that the President has taken a call from Ambassador Power or has called the Ambassador late at night when he is working on a speech because she has agitated to include a controversial component. (Denis McDonough, White House Chief of Staff, cited in Osmos, 2014)

"Serving in the executive branch is very different from sounding off from the academic perch." (Samantha Power, Nomination Hearing, cited in Osmos, 2014)

Early years

Samantha Power appears to be someone as much at home in negotiating positions in an academic as in a political context. She is unorthodox but strategic and establishes deep friendships, including with President Barack Obama, as she moves through both academic and political careers.

Her early years were characterized by her Irish background and move to the US. Power was from a family of doctors and her mother was an Irish sports champion and absorbed by medicine. Her father was a Dublin piano player, raconteur and dentist who enjoyed drinking and who was a formidable debater. Power was very close to her father. Her parents' marriage did not last and her mother met a doctor and the family moved to Pittsburgh, and later to Atlanta, when Power was aged nine. Her father remained in Ireland and died when she was 14. Power became American through baseball and went to Yale as an undergraduate, but was more focused on sports than politics.

Academic career

While at Yale in her freshman year Power was an intern at CBS in Atlanta and became influenced by political developments and turned her attention to history and writing. After she graduated in 1992, as the war in Bosnia expanded, she interned at the Carnegie Endowment for International Peace and accompanied its president, former Assistant Secretary of State Morton Abramowitz, to events.

Power wanted to report from Bosnia but had no experience and the Carnegie Endowment would not back her for a United Nations (UN) credential to travel there. However, she managed to gain entry and in 1993 moved first to Zagreb and then Sarajevo and worked for *The Boston Globe*, *The Washington Post* and *The Economist*. Barbara Demick, who was correspondent for *The Philadelphia Inquirer*, said that 'Samantha was a breath of fresh outrage.' She went on to say that she remembered going into a meeting with Michael Rose who was UN Commander and he said: "'Here comes the 'Bomb the Bastards' bunch". That became their nicknames.'

In 1995 Power enrolled at Harvard Law School and in her second year took a class in the just use of force. As she comments: "I began looking at the historical cases of genocide, looking at the Armenians, the Khmer Rouge, Saddam Hussein ... and Rwanda." She wrote a paper for her class, but also sent it to Anthony Lewis, then a *New York Times* columnist and Martin Perez, who was editing *The New Republic*, both of which followed the Bosnia conflicts. They told her that she should turn it into a book. She took their advice and wrote *A Problem from Hell: America and the Age of Genocide* (2003).

Power's book won the Pulitzer prize and she toured American college campuses drawing large groups of students. *Time* magazine chose her as one of its '100 Most Influential People'. Osmos (2014) notes that Power, in her writing on atrocities, talked about 'a toolbox of interventions'.

He also notes that on the tenth anniversary of the Rwandan genocide she appeared on the *Charlie Rose* show and said 'that the history of inaction held lessons for the U.N. and other organizations'.

In 2005 Power received a dinner invitation from Obama's Senate office. He had read her book and wanted to meet her. Osmos (2014) notes that Power thought that Obama's interest in her book focused on the relationship between systems and outcomes and the misalignment between them. Power felt that Obama had less interest in ideology than in results. She reflects on Obama's motivation and states that 'What he is most interested in is whether the whatever the particular policy tool is likely to produce that outcome that anybody is claiming it is going to produce'. By the end of dinner, Power had proposed taking leave from Harvard to work in Obama's office. She worked for the Obama campaign for the 2008 election.

Service to the administration

Osmos (2014) notes that in 2013 the Senate Foreign Relations committee met to consider the nomination of Samantha Power to be America's Permanent Representative to the UN. Power had served on the NSC as the senior director for multilateral affairs and human rights. At 42 she was the youngest-ever American ambassador to the UN. She had previously campaigned for Barack Obama in 2008 and joined the Obama administration on the NSC in January 2009.

In January 2008, while campaigning for Obama, Power met and started seeing Cass Sunstein, who was then serving as an informal legal advisor to the campaign and was ranked as the most frequently cited legal scholar in America. Sunstein was 16 years older than Power, divorced and had split up with his companion of more than 10 years, the well-known University of Chicago professor Martha Nussbaum. They had become a celebrity academic couple and Sunstein had been long-term friends with Obama since their days of teaching at the University of Chicago. Power and Sunstein were married in July 2008 at a three-day wedding party in Ireland.

During the nomination race between Obama and Hillary Clinton, Power called Clinton 'a monster' because of her criticism of Obama, and this led to considerable strain. It took a friend of Power's, Richard Holbrooke, to intercede in the relationship and this probably saved Power's political career. Holbrooke said that the meeting he brokered between Clinton and Power in Clinton's Manhattan office was 'his wedding present' to Power. Osmos (2014) reports that when Power told Obama about it, he reportedly said, "Gee, most people get toasters". The conciliation was useful, as Clinton became Secretary of State and she and Power worked together on Libyan land-mine policy, women's empowerment and other issues. The relationship was never particularly close.

Power's entry into the Obama administration on the NSC was in January 2009. It was a job involving long hours and limited influence. She had less access to Obama than previously. Kati Marton, an author and Holbrooke's widow, said to Osmos of Power's position: "She did not have a big enough position to throw her weight around but people knew she was Obama's friend, so they couldn't mess with her. She was an upstairs and downstairs, and there are very few others like that." Power's husband, Sunstein, had also been hired and headed the White House Office of Information and Regulatory Affairs, and was nicknamed the government's 'regulatory czar'. The 'power couple' were seen as red flags to the conservative right. As Osmos (2014) comments: 'he attracted obsessive attention from Glen Beck, who called Sunstein and Power "the most dangerous couple in America", subsequent to this Sunstein received death threats'.

Power was seen as an important support person for Obama. When Obama won the Nobel Peace Prize, she worked on several drafts of his speech, which emphasized the justified use of force, arguing that a president can never be Mahatma Gandhi or Martin Luther King, Jr. She began to establish a voice for herself.

Power was hawkish on Libya, arguing for aggressive action, and she, along with Ben Rhodes and Susan Rice, was a strong advocate of getting the US involved in military engagement. However, Robert Gates opposed this. Osmos (2014) maintains that

> The image of Power, Clinton and Rice became a cartoon – Obama's Valkyries leading him to war – but Gates does not believe that Obama ever broadly embraced Power's expansive view of humanitarian intervention. He [Gates] said: 'I think he was being pressurised by the Europeans, particularly the French, the British and Italians, and their interests were much more directly involved than ours. And I think he was much more influenced by that, and by the arguments for preventing this humanitarian disaster, than he was by any kind of broad strategic or philosophical commitment.'

In addition to Libya, Syria was the focus of attention then as now. The Arab Spring was a major factor and reached Syria in 2011, and by the middle of the year Power was arguing in internal White House meetings that arms should be provided to the Syrian opposition forces. The chemical attack by the Assad regime in 2013 resulted in the deaths of more than 1,400 Syrians. Obama raised the prospect of attacking the Assad regime and Power gave a speech at the Centre for American Progress in which she called for military action. There was no strike on Syria. Both Power and Obama were criticized for the lack of action on Syria. Power's critics say that she should have resigned on Syria. Osmos (2014) indicates that 'Jennifer Rubin, a conservative columnist and blogger at the *Washington Post*, accused Power of "simple careerism", writing "staying put doesn't make one noble; it makes one an enabler of the policies one finds despicable".'

Relationship with Susan Rice

Power had to establish relationships with other challenging women in the administration, including Susan Rice. Power was faced with dealing with the disposal of Syria's chemical weapons. Rice, who was Power's predecessor, had become Obama's National Security Adviser and Power needed her support in order to succeed. Power had first encountered Rice, years earlier, under difficult circumstances.

In Power's book on genocide she had quoted Rice, who was then in the Clinton administration, asking colleagues in response to Rwanda: 'if we use the word "genocide" and are seen to be doing nothing, what will be the effect on the November election?' In fact, when Rice was preparing for the Senate confirmation she was asked about the quote in Power's book. Power and Rice became friends and allies and Rice visited her in hospital each time Power had a baby. When Power moved to New York she stayed in close touch with Rice and they worked closely together.

After the re-election of Obama in 2012, Power was nominated for the American ambassadorship at the UN. She skilfully managed to bring both Republicans and Democrats to support her nomination and even persuaded Senator Saxby Chambliss, a Republican from Georgia, to introduce her at the hearing. Despite a tough nomination hearing, she successfully separated her perspective as an academic from that as a member of the executive as follows: "Serving in the executive branch is very different from sounding off from the academic perch." The Senate approved her nomination by 87 votes to 10. After Power was confirmed, Obama spoke at the UN General Assembly. He asked Power to look over his speech and she argued at length for greater emphasis on America's efforts to promote democracy and human rights.

Power is known for pushing unpopular ideas. "People call her activist in chief," said Madeleine Albright, who served as Secretary of State under Bill Clinton. Jake Sullivan, who headed Hillary Clinton's policy-planning staff and later served as Vice-President Joe Biden's national security adviser, said: "More than other individual actors, Samantha is somebody who will encourage, cajole, push and prod the whole system: State Department, Treasury Department, Defense Department."

In her role as American ambassador to the UN, Power had the ambassador's office, which is on the 21st floor of the UN mission on First Avenue in New York, with sweeping views of the East River. Osmos (2014) indicates that

> In a gesture intended to convey humility, Power is trying to meet each of the U.N.'s hundred and ninety three permanent representatives at their offices, instead of hers. Three weeks after she was sworn-in, she visited the two room mission of the Central African Republic, one of the poorest countries in Africa. Six months earlier, Muslim rebels mounted a brutal coup, and anti-Muslim gangs retaliated with wanton bloodshed.

These examples indicate that Power was an unorthodox appointment as American Ambassador to the UN. While in post she took a party of foreign ambassadors to the 9/11 Memorial Museum instead of the more customary visit to watch the Mets or the Knicks play. Her objective was to remind her peers of the human implications of terrorism, as she noted: "It's not a geopolitical strategic abstraction." "It's about groups that attack families who are flying on airplanes, and take the lives of firefighters who are trying to rescue other people."

Publications: books and articles

Power has published a number of significant books and articles and, as noted, her book *A Problem from Hell: America and the Age of Genocide* won the Pulitzer prize and the National Book Critics Circle Award in 2003. She also published the *New York Times* bestseller *Chasing the Flame: Sergio Vieirade Mello and the Fight to Save the World* (2008a) and co-edited with Derek Chollet *The Unquiet American: Richard Holbrooke in the World* (2011). She is currently writing 'The Education of an Idealist', which chronicles her years in public service and reflects the role of human rights and humanitarian ideals in contemporary geopolitics.

Power's journal articles and book chapters are typical of any successful academic and include the following: 'Raising the Cost of Genocide' (2002); 'Introduction to Hannah Arendt, The Origins of Totalitarianism' (2004a); 'Reporting Atrocity: War, Neutrality and the Danger of Taking Sides' (2004b); 'Dying in Dafur' (2005); '"Stopping Genocide and Securing Justice": Learning by Doing – International Justice, War Crimes and Terrorism: The U.S. Record' (2008b); and 'The United States and the Genocide Law: A History of Ambivalence' (2008c).

Contribution and legacy as a public intellectual

Perhaps one of the most interesting aspects of Power's career is the contrast between her ardour as an activist and her duties as an adviser. This has exposed her to the criticism that her commitment to the administration and to her own advancement comes at the expense of her principles and reputation. She remains cautious of the press and media questions and has learnt from 'post-gaffe stress'. An example of this can be found in her appearance on *The Daily Show*. John Stewart asked her a question where she could have made an easy crack about Congress. However, she replied: "We are hopeful that we will see Congress act in support of the effort we are undertaking." This led Stewart to remark: "That was super diplomacy … Ambassadorific."

Power was clearly a significant public intellectual from the publication of her book *'A Problem from Hell': America and the Age of Genocide* and the fact that it won the Pulitzer prize in 2003. Osmos (2014) notes that because of her conviction that America has a responsibility to halt or prevent the suffering of civilians abroad, she has been caricatured as the 'Ivy League Joan of Arc'.

Power has shown herself to be fearless in terms of leading on issues she cares about. She took over as president of the UN Security Council at a time when Ebola virus was posing a threat globally. A Reuters poll in the US found that nearly three-quarters of Americans favoured a ban on flights from the worst-affected areas.

In the face of this, Power decided to visit West Africa to attempt to manage the fears. Osmos (2014) writes that two days before she was due to depart, 'Craig Spencer, an American doctor who had been treating patients in Guinea, tested positive for the virus after returning to New York City. The next day Andrew Cuomo and Chris Christie, the governors of New York and New Jersey, imposed a mandatory quarantine on anyone arriving from West Africa, who had been in contact with ebola patients, even if the traveller had no symptoms.'

Power visited five countries in four days and was determined to generate as many headlines as possible. She hugged people who had recovered from Ebola so that fear could be rationalized, and her intervention provided confidence and challenged irrationality.

Power has learnt that geo-politics requires trade-offs in a way that she was not prepared to concede a decade ago, before joining the Obama administration. Leon Wieseltier, a close friend of Power and Sunstein, saw her as the 'in-house conscience' in the Obama administration:

> "She lifts the President up and reminds him of moral principles and ethical duties and adds a sense of historical grandeur, and won't let him forget the Holocaust and Bosnia and Rwanda and the rest. And I imagine that for Obama it feels so good and so toasty – aren't we really sterling people, and now let's not do anything. This is not saying anything bad about Samantha. Her sincerity and devotion to principle are beyond question. But she plays a certain role in Obama's ecosystem." (cited in Osmos, 2014)

Power's response is as follows:

> "I can be a pain in the ass and that's what he wants. That's what's so amazing. There are plenty of people out there who could check the conscience box". She went on, "There are milder personalities that could create the illusion of inclusion, and spare you the headache of argument and counter-argument, and President Obama did not choose the milder version." (cited in Osmos, 2014)

Susan Rice

> For all those who say she has a reputation as a bare-knuckle fighter, there are others who say it is just the nature of her work and professional passions. (Harris, 2012)

Early years

Susan Rice was born in 1964 in Washington, DC and came from a well-established family who were part of the Washington elite. Her father, Emmet Rice, is a Cornell University economics professor and former governor of the Federal Reserve System. Her mother,

Lois Rice, is an education policy researcher and guest scholar at the Brookings Institution. Rice's family often spoke of politics and foreign policy. Her mother's connections brought in highly prestigious individuals to the house, including Madeleine Albright.

Rice attended the National Catholic School, a preparatory academy in Washington, DC. She excelled in academic subjects, becoming her class valedictorian, and showed an aptitude in the political realm as president of the student council. She was also successful in athletics and became a star player in the basketball team.

Following graduation, Rice attended Stanford University in Palo Alto, California. She was a driven student and excelled. She earned a distinction and also became a Harry S. Truman scholar, was elected to Phi Beta Kappa and earned a Rhodes scholarship. She was also an activist and influenced top administrators when she created a fund that withheld alumni donations until either the university stopped investment in companies doing business in South Africa or the country ended apartheid.

After receiving her bachelor's degree in history in 1986 she went on to attend the University of Oxford. She earned her MPhil and DPhil in international relations and wrote a dissertation that examined Rhodesia's transition from white rule. Her work won the Royal Commonwealth Society's Walter Frewen Lord Prize for outstanding research in the field of Commonwealth history, as well as the Chatham House–British International Studies Association Prize for the most distinguished doctoral dissertation in the UK in the field of international relations.

Rice completed her schooling in 1990. After working in the corporate sector, she married a Canadian Broadcasting Company television producer and in 1993 took up a position with the NSC under President Clinton. She took up the position of special assistant to the president and senior director for African affairs in 1995.

Academic career

Rice left the private sector in 2002 to become a senior fellow in foreign policy for the Brookings Institution, a non-profit public policy organization in Washington, DC. As a fellow, Rice specialized in research on US foreign policy and weak and failing states, as well as the implications of global poverty and transnational security threats. In 2008, Rice took leave from Brookings to become senior foreign policy adviser to Barack Obama during the 2008 election campaign.

Service to the administration

Madeleine Albright was a family friend and long-time mentor to Rice. As stated above, the two families knew one another and Albright helped Rice to get her first job in the administration when, as Harris (2012) comments, 'She catapulted in as head of Africa desk, to the reported annoyance of older African hands and the African press. When she was sworn in, as one of the youngest assistant secretaries of state ever, Albright was reported to have told Rice's mother: "I feel like I'm swearing in family".'

Harris (2012) notes that

> Rice shone in the role which saw her deal with major crises like the bombing of the US embassies in Kenya and Dar es Salaam and bloody conflict in Congo, Eritrea and Ethiopia. "She was a wonderful ambassador for Africa policy. She knows her dossiers, she is hard working and she is sharp", said Professor William Zartman, an Africa expert at Johns Hopkins University who worked with her on African policy.

As noted above, Rice had worked for five years for Bill Clinton at the NSC, specializing in peace keeping and Africa, and working as an advocate for greater intervention. As a result she is tough minded on issues such as intervention in Libya, taking a hard line on Sudan and criticizing China and Russia when they blocked a UN resolution condemning brutality in Syria. Harris (2012) also comments on Rice's ferocious work ethic, such as when she was pregnant with her first child and did not take leave work until the day before the birth.

After Obama's successful election in 2008, Rice was nominated as UN ambassador for the US. In January 2009 she was confirmed by the US Senate, making her the first African-American woman to hold the post. Harris (2012) indicates that she developed a good working relationship with Hillary Clinton, which was not guaranteed, as Rice had supported Obama in 2008.

In her role as US ambassador to the UN 'she [was] seen as a savvy and tough operator who has done much to repair America's status ... She has had a glittering career in foreign affairs via serious roles in the NSC, being America's top diplomat in Africa, and numerous engagements in wonkish think-tank circles' (Harris, 2012). Harris (2012) goes on to say that Rice's many supporters and defenders see her as 'principled, engaged and highly intelligent'. Michael Williams, who is co-editor of *Power in World Politics* and who worked with Rice on the Obama campaign, said of Rice: 'She is a sharp woman. She's Type A. She likes to achieve her goals and she is tireless' (cited in Harris, 2012).

Harris (2012) makes some interesting observations about Rice, indicating that 'she has been a high-flying achiever since high school, racking up an enviable curriculum vitae in academia and practical diplomacy all over the world. But in the viper's nest of Washington D.C., she has now made enemies.' Nor do they seem likely to be placated. This was particularly manifest in the nomination process for the position of Secretary of State to replace Hillary Clinton.

The opposition to Rice's nomination seems to have come partly from her blunt approach as well as her response to the Benghazi episode. Harris (2012) notes that Rice, when she was foreign policy adviser to Obama, verbally attacked the Republican opponent, John McCain, who 'had once donned body armour to visit a Baghdad market on a visit to Iraq'. This was of course a huge insult to McCain and his supporters, who was seen as both a war hero and a man who was brave in the face of adversity.

Apart from this huge diplomatic faux pas, McCain also fiercely opposed Rice over her comments on the Benghazi consulate attack in Libya. Harris (2012) comments: 'While the attack on the Benghazi consulate is the nominal reason for McCain vowing to "do everything" to block Rice, there are some who see personal motivations rooted in an aspect of Rice's personality that has reared its head repeatedly throughout her career: her bluntness.'

The response to Rice's temperament has also come from those less politically opposed. Harris (2012) shows that even the 'influential *Washington Post* columnist, Dana Milbank wrote a scathing piece in which he concluded Obama needed someone with more sensitivity. "Obama can do better at state than Susan Rice", he wrote. The Russians too have been grumbling with anonymous leaks, declaring Rice "too ambitious and too aggressive". In a series of private meetings with Republican senators, including McCain and the moderate Senator Susan Collins, she seems to have produced an even more critical reaction.'

However, there was push-back from others who know her. After Milbank penned his critical piece, one of Rice's former teachers, John Wood, wrote a piece in her defence. He stated: 'I saw "no sharp elbows" whatsoever. In a very demanding school she was laid back, and funny but also focused and hard working' (Harris, 2012). He also pointed out that the school still used the revised honour code that Rice had drawn up three decades earlier.

Indeed Harris (2012) maintains that 'For all those who say she has a reputation as a bare-knuckle fighter, there are others who say it is just the nature of her work and professional passions.' In fact Harris says that some believe the political sniping has a lot to do with sexism: few male political figures are criticized for aggression. The Republicans as a political block opposed Rice's nomination. Harris (2012) is more critical of Obama for his lack of an effective foreign policy. Professor Aaron Miller, a vice-president of the Woodrow Wilson Centre said of Obama: 'Barack Obama became a less ideological but more effective version of George W. Bush.' Harris commented in 2012 that no one thought Rice would change that. She was known as being close to Obama and less likely to be able to push back. She was seen as tough and sharp but followed orders.

Rice was successful in the role of UN ambassador, gaining UN approval for sanctions against Iran and North Korea and military action in Libya. However, she was criticized following the September 2012 attack on two American facilities in Benghazi in Libya. Rice appeared in the media and said that the attack was the result of a video shown on the internet. However, it was later shown to be a highly planned and executed attack by extremists.

National security adviser

Rice was made national security adviser in the Obama administration in 2013, following Tom Donilon. President Obama expressed his delight at working with her again: "I am absolutely thrilled that she'll be back at my side, leading my national security team in my second term" (cited in Osmos, 2014).

Rice was highly effective in the role and oversaw the coordination of intelligence and military efforts during a period that was marked by an escalation of the battle against the Islamic State of Iraq and Syria (ISIS) in the Middle East, the crisis in Syria and increased aggression from Russia. She shared the president's view on withholding large troop deployment to the Middle East and a focus on the containment of nuclear Iran.

However, this period was also characterized by controversy as – although her role ended in 2017 – she became involved in the ongoing controversy of Russian interference during the 2016 presidential campaign and the investigation of the Trump campaign's collusion with the Russians. This is of course still being investigated as I complete this book, under Special Counsel Robert Mueller, despite the ongoing attacks by Trump and his administration to avoid impeachment or indictment.

Trump attacked Rice in April 2017 after he levied accusations of 'wire-tapping' of Trump Tower by the Obama administration. Trump accused Rice of leaking the identities of Americans caught up in the electronic surveillance of foreign officials. Rice denied the accusations and said that everything she was doing was within the jurisdiction of the NSC. The investigation continues into the Trump campaign.

Graham (2017a), in an article in *The Atlantic* entitled 'Did Susan Rice Do Anything Wrong by Asking to "Unmask" Trump Officials?', maintains that the issue of the surveillance arose after the activities of Devin Nunes, Republican chairman of the House Intelligence Committee. In reporting on the story, *Bloomberg View*'s Eli Lake wrote that 'White House lawyers last month discovered that the former national security adviser Susan Rice requested the identities of U.S. persons in raw intelligence reports on dozens of occasions that connect to the Donald Trump transition and campaign according to U.S. officials familiar with the matter' (Lake, 2017).

There is of course no evidence that anything Rice did was illegal, and in fact Graham (2017a) comments that there is a possibility that Rice was acting in conjunction with a joint investigation into Russian meddling in the election including Paul Manafort and other aides. It would not be unusual for a national security adviser to attempt to understand the actions of a foreign government. The problem is that Rice is reviled and distrusted by the Republicans because of Benghazi. This issue has now been taken over by the Special Counsel investigation led by Robert Mueller, showing that Rice's concerns were justified, despite Trump's hostility and objections to the investigation.

The partisan response to Rice is shown by Graham (2017b) in an article entitled 'Why Won't Susan Rice Testify to Congress?' in *The Atlantic*. Senator Lindsey Graham called for her to appear in front of the Senate Sub-Committee on Crime and Terrorism in 2017, but she refused. This was to discuss the issue of improper unmasking. She insisted that this had not been done for political reasons. By declining to testify, Rice appeared to look as if she was hiding something.

As regards Trump's allegation that he and Trump Tower in New York had been the subject of surveillance ordered by President Obama prior to the election, Rice had the following response: "There was no collection or surveillance on Trump Tower or Trump individuals, and by that I mean directed by the White House or targeted at Trump individuals" (cited in Graham, 2017a).

In an article by Jeffrey Goldberg (2017) in *The Atlantic* entitled "'The Autocratic Element": Can America Ever Recover from the Trump Administration?', Goldberg interviewed the editor of *The Atlantic*, David Frum. Goldberg asked about the idea of pursuing criminal charges against the losing candidate (Hillary Clinton) in the 2016 presidential contest. Frum 'called this pursuit "sinister" but then pointed me to something he considered even more pernicious: the quest to punish former National Security Adviser, Susan Rice, for "unmasking" people associated with Trump's campaign whose communications with foreign officials were captured during the US intelligence collection, and they're pursuing her for this.' Frum went on to say: "It is not merely that they are trying to use the mechanisms of the law to attack political opponents; it is that they are trying to use the power of the state to conceal, through diversion by an autocratic government, an attempt to steal an American election."

Conclusion

The three women public intellectuals, Condoleezza Rice, Samantha Power and Susan Rice, are significant role models for women wanting to move from academic positions into different administrations. Slaughter (2012) (see Chapter Seven) maintains that these women cannot be held up as role models, as they are brilliant scholars and thinkers and pose unrealistic models for women. This is not a view I would subscribe to, as none of these women was born into privilege or benefited particularly from connections. They made their own success through a meritocratic environment, outstanding commitment and hard work. They are very much the models that are required and exactly the models of women public intellectuals that we need to see.

Contemporary women public intellectuals: the United States (2)

Introduction

Chapter Seven continues the themes developed in Chapter Six and explores the position of contemporary women public intellectuals and considers initially the issue of whether women successfully combine a high-level and demanding political or corporate life with a family life. This is particularly an issue for women with children. The question is posed in the context of an article written by Anne-Marie Slaughter, a highly successful and experienced academic who moved into the administration to serve under Secretary of State Hillary Clinton and who outlines some of the challenges for women of combining political roles with family life. Slaughter (2012) draws on the experiences of three women in particular in outlining her case: Elizabeth Warren, Hillary Clinton and Sheryl Sandberg. This chapter examines how all three women fared as public intellectuals in the context of contemporary political and corporate life.

Anne-Marie Slaughter is president of the New America Foundation and is the Bert G. Kerstetter '66 University Professor of Politics and International Affairs at Princeton University. She was previously Director of Policy Planning for the US State Department under Hillary Clinton and the dean of Princeton's Woodrow Wilson School of Public and International Affairs. She was the first woman director of policy planning at the State Department, taking a two-year public service leave from Princeton University.

In a startling article in *The Atlantic* magazine in 2012, entitled 'Why Women Still Can't Have it All', Slaughter sets out the issues for women who have moved from academic life into the administration in Washington, DC and how this impacts on family life. Given her high-profile positions in academic and corporate life, her article and subsequent decisions surprised and indeed shocked women who are attempting to balance career aspirations with a family life. As Slaughter (2012: 3) comments: 'I routinely got reactions from other women my age and older that ranged from disappointed ("It's a pity that you had to leave Washington") to condescending ("I wouldn't generalise from your experience. I've never had to compromise and my kids turned out great").'

In her article, Slaughter sets out the differences between academic and political life, at least in the US, saying that she spent her career in academia as a law professor and then as a dean. She comments that both positions were demanding but she had the ability to set her own schedule most of the time. By contrast, her time in Washington was characterized by the demands of a 'rigid bureaucracy', as Slaughter (2012: 6) comments:

> I spent two years in Washington within a rigid bureaucracy even with bosses as understanding as Hillary Clinton and her chief of staff, Cheryl Mills. My working week started at 4.20am on Monday morning, when I got up to get the 5.30am train from Trenton to Washington … It ended late on Friday with the train home. In between the days were crammed with meetings, and when the meetings stopped, the writing work began – a never ending stream of memos, reports and comments on other people's drafts. For two years I never left the office early enough to go to any stores other than those open 24 hours, which meant that everything from dry cleaning to hair appointments to Christmas shopping had to be done on weekends, amid children's sporting events, music lessons, family meals and conference calls.

As Slaughter comments, Secretary Clinton would arrive in the office at 8am and leave around 7pm, to allow her staff to have mornings and evenings with their families. The long hours, which of course were extended at home, meant that 'having it all' could not be achieved.

While the emphasis in the media is always on the 'high-flyers' and success stories in Washington, DC, there are a number of successful women who have made decisions to focus on family at certain points rather than on career. Slaughter (2012: 7) notes that Michele Flournoy stepped down after three years as undersecretary of defense for policy to spend more time at home. Karen Hughes left her position as counsellor to President George W. Bush after a year and a half in Washington. Mary Matalin spent two years as an assistant to President George W. Bush and counsellor to Vice-President Dick Cheney before stepping down to spend more time with her daughters.

Slaughter (2012) comments that she has only just begun to realize the extent to which many young professional women feel under assault by women who are older and who have achieved a great deal of success. Younger women feel pressured by more senior women, as they feel under pressure to perform at a higher level.

Interestingly, Slaughter (2012: 9) comments on an address by Sheryl Sandberg, Facebook's chief operating officer, in her 2011 commencement speech at Barnard College. In this address Sandberg maintains there is an 'ambition gap' for younger women and that women do not dream big enough.

> [S]he lamented the dismally small number of women at the top and advised young women not 'to leave before you leave'. "When a woman starts blinking about having children", Sandberg said, "she does not raise her hand anymore … She starts leaning back". Although couched in terms of encouragement, Sandberg's exhortation contains more than a note of reproach. We who have made it to the top, or are striving to get there, are essentially saying to the women in the generation behind us: "What's the matter with you?" (Slaughter, 2012: 9)

The issue raised by these debates is that they address a fairly privileged demographic of highly educated and well-off women who have the economic resources and social capital to make choices. Slaughter (2012: 11) argues:

> The best hope for improving the lot of all women and for closing what Wolfers and Stevenson call a 'new gender gap' measured by well-being rather than wages – is to close the leadership gap: to elect a woman president and 50 women senators, to ensure that women are equally represented in the ranks of corporate executives and judicial leaders. Only when women wield power in sufficient numbers will we create a society that genuinely works for all women.

Slaughter somewhat dauntingly claims that women who make it to the top positions are 'genuine superwomen'. As she says:

> Consider the number of women recently in the top ranks in Washington – Susan Rice, Elizabeth Sherwood-Randall, Michele Gavin, Nancy-Ann Min de Parle – who are

Rhodes Scholars. Samantha Power, another senior White House official won a Pulitzer Prize at age 32. Or consider Sandberg herself, who graduated with the prize given at Harvard to top students of economics. (Slaughter, 2012: 12)

Slaughter argues that we cannot draw on these women as the standard against which even very talented professional women can measure themselves, as establishing such a standard sets up most women for a sense of failure. She also points out that when children are added into the equation, the level of disadvantage becomes clearer. Slaughter points out that in the Supreme Court all the male Supreme Court justices have a family, whereas two of the three female justices are single with no children. The third, Ruth Bader Ginsburg, began her career only when her younger child was almost grown-up. Slaughter shows that the same is true of the NSC: Condoleezza Rice is the first and only woman national security adviser since the 1950s not to have a family.

Zenko (2011, 2012), in his research on the representation of women in different spheres of government including foreign policy, national security, academia and think-tanks, shows that women are significantly underrepresented. Juliette Kayyem, who served as assistant secretary in the Department of Homeland Security from 2009 to 2011 and is a regular media contributor, told Zenko (2012) that

> "the basic truth is also this: the travel sucks. As my youngest of three children is now 6, I can look back at the years when they were all young and realize how disruptive all the travel was. There were also trips I couldn't take because I was pregnant or on leave, the conferences I couldn't attend because … kids would be home from school, and the various excursions that were offered but just couldn't be managed."

Slaughter (2012: 10), in an open critique of Sandberg's 'lack of ambition' comment, argues that 'the need to travel constantly to succeed, the conflicts between school schedules, the insistence that work is done in the office – cannot be solved by exhortations to close the ambition gap'. Slaughter (2012: 10) comments in a direct critique of Sandberg's speech: 'I would hope to see commencement speeches that finger America's social and business policies rather than women's level of ambition, in explaining the dearth of women at the top. But changing those policies requires much more than speeches.'

Slaughter talks about the practical strategies to make the work–life balance more flexible, such as working from home and state-of-the-art video-conferencing facilities that can drastically reduce the need for long business trips. Slaughter (2012: 26) gives a number of examples of high-profile, hugely successful women who have managed a work–life balance:

> Cheryl Mills, Hillary Clinton's indefatigable chief of staff, has twins in elementary school; even with a fully engaged husband, she famously gets up at 4am every morning to check and send emails before her kids wake up. Louise Richardson now vice chancellor of the University [of Oxford] … combined an assistant professorship in government in Harvard with mothering three young children.

Elizabeth Warren has a similar story. When she had two young children and a part-time law practice, she struggled to find enough time to write the papers and articles that would help her get an academic position.

As Slaughter (2012: 29) comments, because of the changing age-demographic profile for women and men,

> a professional woman can thus expect her working life to stretch some 50 years, from her early or mid-20s to her mid-70s. It is reasonable to assume that she will build her credentials and establish herself, at least in her first career, between 22 and 35; she will have children if she wants them, sometime between 25 and 45; she'll want maximum flexibility and control over her time in the 10 years that her children are 8 to 18; and she should plan to take positions of maximum authority and demands on her time after her children are out of the house.

In addition, women can expect to reach the top later than previously:

> Women who have children in their later 20s can expect to immerse themselves completely in their careers in their late 40s with plenty of time still to rise to the top in their late 50s and early 60s. Women who make partner, managing director, or senior vice president, get tenure, or establish a medical practice before having children in their late 30s,

should be coming back on line for the most demanding jobs at almost exactly the same age. (Slaughter, 2012: 29)

Peaking in your late 50s and early 60s rather than your late 40s and early 50s makes particular sense for women who live longer than men. And many of the stereotypes about older workers simply do not hold. A 2006 survey of human resources professionals shows that only 23 percent think older workers are less flexible than younger workers; only 11 percent think older workers require more training than younger workers; and only 7 percent think older workers have less drive than younger workers. (Slaughter, 2012: 30)

Slaughter also notes that some institutions are slowly moving to changes in policy:

[I]n 1970, Princeton established a tenure-extension policy that allowed female assistants professors expecting a child to request a one-year extension to their tenure clocks. This policy was later extended to men, and broadened to include adoptions. In the early 2000s, two reports on the status of female faculty discovered that only 3 percent of assistant professors requested tenure extensions in any given year. And in response to a survey question, women were much more likely than men to think that a tenure extension would be detrimental to an assistant professor's career. (Slaughter, 2012: 30)

In 2005, under President Shirley Tilghman, Princeton changed the default rule. The administration announced that all assistant professors, female and male, who had a new child would automatically receive a one-year extension on the tenure check, with no opt-outs allowed. Instead assistant professors could request early consideration for tenure if they wished. The number of assistant professors who receive a tenure extension has tripled since the change. (Slaughter, 2012: 31)

Slaughter makes the important point that when women are in power they can help to change the university environment. As Slaughter (2012: 33) herself notes, women in power can and should change that environment, although change is not easy. When I became dean of the Woodrow Wilson School in 2002 I decided that one of the advantages of being a woman in power was that I could help change the norms by deliberately talking about my children and my desire to have a balanced life. Thus I would end faculty meetings at 6pm by saying that I had to go home for dinner; I would also make clear to all student organizations that I would not come to dinner with them because I needed to be home from six to eight, but that I would often be willing to come back after eight for a meeting. I also told the Dean's Advisory Committee that the associate dean would chair the next session so I could go to a parent-teacher conference.

Actually the response of some of the women academics was to criticize Slaughter's approach and to tell her to stop talking about her kids, as they felt that Slaughter was not showing the 'gravitas' required of a dean and that, as she was the first woman dean, she needed to convey a different identity. Slaughter told them that she was emphasizing the point for effect, but she said that she found it interesting that these junior academics did not equate gravitas with parenthood and what it entailed.

Sheryl Sandberg (see below) is famous for acknowledging that she leaves work at 5.30pm to have dinner with her family. She also readily admits that for many years she did not admit to this, despite the fact that she would have made up the time elsewhere or later in the evening.

It is of course not only women who see the need for change in the work–life balance, and Slaughter cites Martha Minow, dean of the Harvard Law School, who argues that over 30 years of teaching law at Harvard she observes that many young men are asking questions about how to manage work–life balance.

In conclusion, Slaughter (2012: 41) comments: 'If women are ever to achieve real equality as leaders, then we have to stop accepting male behaviour and male choices as default and the ideal. We must insist on changing social policies and bending career tracks to accommodate our choices too.'

So we can now look at the way in which three of the women public intellectuals discussed by Slaughter have negotiated their position in political and economic life. These are: Elizabeth Warren, Sheryl Sandberg and Hillary Clinton.

Elizabeth Warren

'Pocahontas'. This is the racially charged term that Trump used on the campaign trail to dismiss Warren, who has claimed Native American heritage. The Massachusetts senator was a self-declared 'nasty woman' with a message for Trump: 'Women have had it with guys like you'. She went toe to toe with him on his favourite medium, Twitter, hammering him for delivering a '"one-two" punch of bigotry and economic lies'. (Smith, 2017)

Reviewing Warren's book for *The New York Times*, economist Paul Krugman wrote: 'Let's be honest: Republicans have gone after Warren herself, in a way they haven't gone after Sanders, in part because of her gender.' (Smith, 2017)

Early years

Elizabeth Warren has always used her biography as a political statement and as a means of identifying with the day-to-day struggles of ordinary Americans. She proudly offered the following summary of her background:

"I grew up in a family on the ragged edge of the middle class. My daddy sold carpeting and ended up as a maintenance man. After he had a heart attack, my mom worked the phones at Sears so we could hang on to our house. My three brothers all served in the military. One was career. The second worked a good union job in construction. The third started a small business. … I was waiting tables at 13 and married at 19. I graduated from public school and taught elementary school. I have a wonderful husband, two great children and three beautiful grandchildren. I am grateful down to my toes for every opportunity that America gave me." (Warren, cited in Nair, 2013)

Academic profile

The emphasis on Warren's background as she presents it does not tend to focus on her academic profile, which has been a significant part of her life. Warren has been a prominent academic since the late

1970s and is well known for her work in bankruptcy law. Warren graduated from the University of Houston with a BSc in Science in 1970 and received her Juris Doctorate (JD) from Rutgers School of Law–Newark in 1976. From 1977 to 1987 she taught at the University of Houston Law Centre and the University of Texas, School of Law. From 1987 to 1995 she was a tenured professor at the University of Pennsylvania Law School. In 1992 Warren worked at Harvard Law School as a visiting professor and in 1995 she received a permanent appointment as the Leo Gottlieb Professor of Law, Harvard Law School. She has taught in several areas of financial law, including bankruptcy, contracts, secured lending, corporations and partnerships. Nair (2013) maintains that her academic record offers insights into her philosophy and core values:

> Despite her significant role in academia, Warren is a critic of the ivory tower approach to financial policy. She, like Samantha Power, is critical of the lack of a real world approach to financial theories. Her position is that bankruptcy is directly related to external forces rather than consumer irresponsibility. Obama strongly supported Warren's position.

Service to the administration

Warren used her economic stance as a major part of her focus of her Senate campaign and she has also been influential in her contribution to debates on affordable health-care and college debt. She is of course, along with Bernie Sanders, seen as a progressive. Green (2017), in an article in *The Washington Post* entitled 'After 2016's losses Elizabeth Warren tells Democrats: "Shame on Us"', focuses on what she sees as [Hillary] 'Clinton's shocking failure'. As Green (2017) comments: 'In her retelling of the elections that left Republicans in control of the White House, Congress, 32 statehouses and 33 governor's mansions, Warren styles herself as a populist Cassandra who expected Trump's victory. In addition, Clinton earns no praise for her policies or leadership – Warren subtly suggests that her endorsement was more practical than ideological.'

Perhaps one of the most significant events of her time in the Senate so far has been her clash with Mitch McConnell in the Senate chamber. Garber (2017), in an article in *The Atlantic*, '"Nevertheless She Persisted" and the Age of the Weaponised Meme', outlines how Warren established herself as a force to be reckoned with.

As Warren was reading the words of Coretta Scott King, widow of Martin Luther King, in the Senate, she was interrupted by another senator and then by Mitch McConnell who attempted to silence her, saying: "She was warned, she was given an explanation. Nevertheless she persisted". As a result there was a *Twitter* storm around 'Silencing Liz Warren' and '# Let Liz speak' as well as '#She persisted'. This was also applied to images of: Harriet Tubman, Malala Yousafzai, Beyoncé, Emmeline Pankhurst, Gaby Gifford, Michelle Obama and Hillary Clinton. It was also reported widely in social media.

In another article in *The Atlantic*, entitled 'A Triumphant Moment for Elizabeth Warren', Foran (2017) comments that

> It was a triumphant moment for Warren, who has cultivated an image as an unwavering liberal champion, and progressive organizations raced to rally around her. MoveOn.org, Our Revolution, the group founded from the ashes of Bernie Sanders' presidential campaign and Democracy for America all took to social media to show solidarity with Warren, while the hashtags #LetLizSpeak and #ShePersisted quickly went viral.

Warren's reputation has been built on her role as a 'progressive fighter' and comes from her track record of opposition to Trump, which goes back to before his presidency. She continued to be extremely outspoken about him during the 2016 presidential campaign and rallied Democrats against him.

Warren, democracy and Trump

In her new book, *This Fight is Our Fight* (2017), Warren recalls on Inauguration Day seeing protestors carrying a banner with the word 'FASCIST'. When asked if she sees Trump as an authoritarian, she replies: "Look at what he has done. He has expressed his admiration for Mussolini, for Vladimir Putin. He has tried to undermine a free press. He's shown no respect for the courts. Those are the steps that authoritarians take" (cited in Smith, 2017).

Hillary Clinton has frequently said that she felt misogyny was a factor in her defeat. When he reviewed Warren's book for *The New York Times*, Paul Krugman said: 'Let's be honest: Republicans have gone after Warren ... in a way they haven't gone after Sanders, in part because of her gender' (Krugman, 2017).

Sheryl Sandberg

> Sandberg's prominent perch in the male-dominated tech world is central to the promise of *Lean In*. Read this book, follow my lead, get ahead. Throughout the book, Sandberg carefully weighs the double binds, internal and external that keep women from reaching their potential in the workplace. Then she dispatches personal anecdotes, to become, as a Forbes article once anointed her, the fifth most powerful woman in the world. (Hess, 2013)

> "I know that some believe that by focusing on what women can do to change themselves – pressing them to lean in – it seems that I am letting our institutions off the hook." (Sandberg, cited in Williams, 2013)

Early career

Sandberg had a stunning academic profile long before she was associated with Facebook and Mark Zuckerberg. She was born in 1969 and gained a bachelor's degree at Harvard in Economics. Lawrence (Larry) Summers was her thesis adviser. She studied the role that economics played in spousal abuse and founded a group called Women in Economics and Government, which Sandberg says was created 'to get more women to major in government and economics'. She graduated in 1991 and when Summers became the World Bank's chief economist he asked her to be one of his research assistants. Sandberg worked for Summers for two years and then returned to the Harvard Business School, attaining an MBA and graduating with distinction in 1995.

Administration and corporate life

Summers became Deputy Treasury Secretary in the Clinton administration and asked Sandberg to become his chief of staff. Sandberg remained in post when Summers became Secretary to the Treasury in 1999. After the loss of the administration to the Republicans, Sandberg moved into corporate life.

In 2000 Sandberg moved to Silicon Valley to work for Google. She was then persuaded by Mark Zuckerberg to join Facebook, where she has been chief operating officer since 2008. She became the first female member of the Facebook board of directors in 2012.

Publications, contribution and legacy

Sandberg is a bestselling author and her books and the controversy surrounding them have framed her contribution and legacy. Her books include *Lean In* and *Women, Work and the Will to Lead*. Unlike other women public intellectuals with distinct academic careers and hugely successful publications, winning Pulitzer prizes, Sandberg does not write as an academic but as a corporate thinker who is interested in the advancement of women in corporate life. Perhaps Sandberg's greatest contribution and legacy is the ongoing debate around whether or not her books address the position of women generally and whether her views can be seen as a contribution to feminism.

On the issue of Sandberg's feminism (or lack of it), Sommers (2013) comments that her book *Lean In* (2013) 'is mired in 1970s-style feminism'. *The Nation* magazine columnist Kate Pollitt compares Sandberg to 'someone who has taken Women's Studies 101 and wants to share with friends' (Sommers, 2013).

Some have been far more scathing about Sandberg's contribution to feminism and as a feminist. Foster (2016a), in an article in the *Guardian* entitled 'Sheryl Sandberg and Christine Lagarde Have Done Nothing to Advance Feminism', argues that:

> High profile women are still a rarity, and as Sandberg points out in her book, *Lean In*, she got there as did many of her female peers, by aping the behaviour and careers of high-profile men. Rather than change the system, they've colluded with it, and propped it up by appealing to others to do so, suggesting that this is possible for all women.

In fact, Foster (2016b) wrote *Lean Out* to counter the move towards an individualist approach to feminism 'which considers successes by particular women as intrinsically feminist to the detriment of women's economic and social position in society'. Potts (2015), in an article in the *Daily Beast* entitled 'Why Do Feminists Hate Sheryl Sandberg So Much?', raises the question of why feminist are so critical of Sandberg: 'Sandberg is perceived to be writing about and working to address challenges faced by a small group of elite women, those who have piled up the fancy degrees, racked up experience in the corporate world, and arguably should be shattering the glass ceiling into a million little pieces but are not.' The journalist Sarah Leonard told *The New Yorker*'s Vauhini Vara that "The fact that she has more efficiently rallied corporate leaders of both genders around the campaign than she has rallied women of different socioeconomic classes is very telling about who the campaign is for" (cited in Potts, 2015).

Writing in *The New Republic*, Elizabeth Bruenig (2015) went even further and argued that the way Sandberg conducts her campaigns risks hurting lower-waged women, as she comments: 'Sandberg's corporate feminism preaches individual female empowerment in the workplace (and now at home, too) rather than collective social action … and women who subscribe to that approach are more likely to funnel resources into advanced education and leadership training, rather than into the machinery of politics and protest.'

In addition, North (2013), writing in *Buzz Feed* in an article entitled 'The Case for Trickle Up Feminism', argues that 'Feminism is a movement founded on women's status as a marginalized group … and as a woman moves closer to the centres of corporate or government power, she can come to seem like, for lack of a better word, the man.'

An extreme critique of Sandberg's 'old style' feminist perspective comes from the ever critical Camille Paglia, whose comments are cited in Zilber (2017). Paglia criticized Sandberg for her *Lean In* book as being an example of the 'excessively bourgeois or white middle class assumptions of much feminist thought today'.

In a more balanced assessment of Sandberg's book, Valenti (2013), writing in *The Washington Post*, argues that

> Sheryl Sandberg isn't the perfect feminist. So what? Sandberg has been called out of touch, her book 'a vanity project'. She's been slammed as being too interested in building her brand and for advising women on work and family issues while having the temerity to employ a nanny.

Valenti acknowledges the shortcomings of *Lean In* – that it is directed at married women with children, which is of course the Sandberg benchmark, and may not resonate with women with committed careers, or women who aren't upper middle-class or elite – and in fairness Sandberg recognizes this. Valenti also comments on the fact that critics have focused on a critique of Sandberg that emphasizes the fact that she puts the onus on women to lift themselves up rather than providing criticisms of society and sexism. Valenti points out that in her book Sandberg frequently identifies both internal and external factors that hamper women from advancing in their careers, including the need for structural change, economic inequalities, discrimination, lack of paid maternity leave and affordable childcare as factors that need to be addressed.

There is endless criticism of Sandberg by writers who demean their own position in doing so. A prime example is Maureen Dowd (2013), who, in a *New York Times* article entitled 'Pompom Girl for Feminism', calls Sandberg the 'Power Point Pied Piper in Prada Ankle Boots', which smacks of resentfulness at Sandberg's success and offers little in the way of scholarly insight into her thinking.

If this was the case, why was the same criticism not made of Tina Brown when she moved from *Vanity Fair* to *The New Yorker* and, with two young kids, recruited her mother from the UK to provide childcare service?

As Valenti (2013) accurately comments:

> The view that Sandberg is too rich and powerful to advise working women is short-sighted. It assumes that any sort of success is antithetical to feminism. The cutting down of feminist leaders is nothing new ... 'trashing' within the feminist movement has become a toxic yet accepted form of policing other feminists especially those perceived as successful.

And Valenti (2013) is correct when she recognizes that Sandberg's elite networks can be valuable for all women, as she notes: 'Few of us host dinners for Nobel prize winners or count former Treasury secretaries among our mentors ... Sandberg's power as an evangelist and organiser of American elites is profound. Like it or not, a social justice movement needs power behind it – on the ground and from the boardroom.'

Sandberg's approach is not a feminist one as understood from an academic perspective but is a corporate feminist perspective from an executive who is rich, successful and has the resources to employ nannies. But this should not result in a dismissal of her views, which are individualist and not collectivist. Rather than providing a collectivist 'one size fits all' feminism, she, as Potts (2015) indicates, 'speaks directly to women about the ways in which they internalize sexism and lower expectations for themselves in the workplace'.

There is an entire generation of women who trivialize feminism, do not understand feminism and have largely rejected it, so we cannot dismiss Sandberg's view of basic feminist strategies. Potts (2015) disagrees with the critique of Sandberg and says that she feels Sandberg's perspective is not only for elite women, or that it does not inspire a sense of 'in-it-togetherness'. As Potts (2015) comments:

Sandberg's biggest contribution ... She gave women permission to talk about their work, to take pride in it, and to admit they wanted to be successful. In most of America's society women are still required to view their roles as mothers first. Subtle grooming of women to lower their academic and professional expectations so that they are not let down or pulled away from home or family, the disdain with which men openly disregard the work women do at home – those beliefs are more prevalent than many would like to believe in 2015.

Hillary Clinton

I go back over my shortcomings and the mistakes we made. I take responsibility for all of them. You can blame the data, blame the message, blame anything you want but I was the candidate. It was my campaign. Those were my decisions. (Clinton, 2017)

I was running a traditional presidential campaign with careful thought out policies and painstakingly built coalitions, while Trump was running a reality TV show that expertly and relentlessly stoked American's anger and resentment. I was giving speeches laying out how to solve the country's problems. He was ranting on *Twitter*. (Clinton, 2017)

It can be excruciating, humiliating. The moment a woman steps forward and says 'I'm running for office', it begins, the analysis of her face, her body, her voice, her demeanour, the diminishment of her stature, her ideas, her accomplishments, her integrity. (Clinton, 2017)

I end this book with the woman who is probably the most famous woman public intellectual on the planet, Hillary Clinton. She has come closest to breaking the 'glass ceiling' in US politics and has provided signposts for women, both positive and negative, about what it means to be a woman at the highest levels of the public sphere. Sadly, as a result of Clinton's failure to win the presidency, the US is left in a position where it has to tolerate the demeaning experience of suffering the Trump presidency. But this will be a short-lived experience, which will undoubtedly end badly, through impeachment or resignation or other, and there are many excellent women on both sides of the divide who could stand – Elizabeth Warren, Michelle Obama, Nicky Haley – waiting in the wings. Because Hillary Clinton was in the White House as First Lady, I have modified some of the sections to include that.

Early years

Bernstein (2007, 2016) is widely regarded as Hillary Rodham Clinton's definitive biographer. He describes three pillars that define the life of Hillary Clinton: family, religion and public service. Bernstein claims that this defines everything she does. Her Methodism defines her life and her politics, and Bernstein notes that she carries a Bible with her and reads it in cars and on planes.

Bernstein shows that Clinton's father was the worst part of her childhood, particularly his abuse of her mother. He was verbally abusive and showed diminution and disdain towards her mother. Bernstein (2016: 3) records Clinton's recollection of how her father spoke to her mother as follows: "What do you know Miss Fancypants? You don't have anything to contribute to this." And, as Bernstein notes, he would go on diminishing her and she would get emotionally upset and leave the table. And then he would say: "Go ahead, just don't let the screen door hit your ass on the way out." Hillary's mother taught her to stand up against men. Her father was supportive of Hillary but harsh in his expectations of her. He tried to restrict her learning to drive, as well as going on dates.

Traister (2016) comments that in 1947, when Clinton was born, there were no women serving in the Senate, and notes that Clinton remembers, as a girl, running home from her suburban Chicago primary school on Fridays to read *Life* magazine, which is where she discovered Margaret Chase Smith, the first woman elected to both houses of Congress, and was just amazed that this woman did this.

Academic profile

Bill Clinton is often seen as the intellectual force in the relationship between Hillary and Bill Clinton, but she had a successful and above-average academic profile before her life collided directly with Bill Clinton, politics and administrations.

Hillary Clinton attended Wellesley College and soon established herself as a young public intellectual. She was well known before she met Bill. Bernstein (2016: 5) outlines her profile academically and politically. She graduated from Wellesley in 1969 and had given a commencement address at the height of the anti-war movement that drew national attention to her. The students had chosen her to deliver the speech as she was president of her class. Her speech, which was supportive of young people as supporters of the anti-war movement, earned her national recognition, as Bernstein (2016: 5) comments:

> The speech drew tremendous response, and resonated in the press, and *Life* magazine featured a profile of her very prominently. So when Bill Clinton met Hillary at Yale Law School, he knew who she was. She was famous, and there had been stories about how she was going to move ahead in the political process and maybe be President of the United States someday.

After meeting Bill Clinton at Yale Law School in 1970, Hillary had intended to stay in Washington, DC after working on the House Judiciary Committee's Nixon impeachment investigation. But she failed the bar exams and so, rather than staying in Washington, she joined Bill Clinton in Arkansas and her political and administrative career began. Traister (2016) comments as follows:

> By the time she graduated from Yale Law School, many people, including her boyfriend Bill, believed she could, and should, embark on a political career. She'd given the Wellesley commencement address speech that had earned her a *Life* write-up of her own. She had volunteered for New Haven's legal services clinic, worked on Walter Mondale's subcommittee investigating the living and working conditions of migrant labourers, spent a year accompanying doctors on rounds at Yale New Haven Hospital researching child abuse, and began work for her future mentor and boss Marian Wright Edelman. In 1973 she would publish a well-regarded paper on children's legal rights and in 1974, she worked for the committee to impeach Richard Nixon.

When in Arkansas, she immediately took action to begin building a women's movement in the state that included rape crisis centres and opportunities in politics for women, and she also used her maiden name. Bill lost the election for state governor and Hillary took over and became the architect of his political career, 'planning the battle to regain the governorship in two years, persuading Bill to adopt more flexible, pragmatic positions on issues' (Bernstein, 2016: 7).

> Political possibilities for women were expanding, slowly, Margaret Chase Smith had run for president in 1964, Shirley Chisholm in 1972. In 1984, Walter Mondale named Geraldine Ferraro as his running mate. 'That was a big moment for me', said Clinton. 'I was at the convention because Bill was governor. And it was so thrilling'. She took Chelsea to meet Ferraro when she came to Little Rock to campaign. (Bernstein, 2016: 7)

Throughout the time in Arkansas and beyond, Bill Clinton had affairs that Hillary was well aware of. After she arrived in Arkansas, he had an affair with a student volunteer. Hillary ran the young woman off campaign headquarters, but his political opponents were already waging a whispering campaign against him. A more serious affair occurred towards the end of his gubernatorial period in Arkansas. However, realizing that Hillary would fight for the marriage, Bill decide to not leave. Hillary continually supported Bill publicly during these times. As this is the story of Hillary Clinton as a public intellectual I have not spent time in outlining the multiple affairs Bill Clinton engaged in and that Hillary Clinton tolerated.

Administrations/First Lady/political futures

Bernstein says that Hillary's support for Bill saved him. Bernstein sees the Clinton presidency as a 'co-presidency'. He notes that the presidency covered areas such as economic policy, health and women's rights and foreign policy. They established themselves as 'outside' the Washington establishment, which did not win them any friends.

When the Monica Lewinsky affair led to the impeachment of Bill Clinton, he did not think his presidency would survive the first week of the scandal. Once again, Hillary saved him by going on the *Today* show and giving 'connubial credence' to his denials, thus saving his presidency.

After the Lewinsky affair and the failed Republican attempt to get Bill Clinton impeached, the Republicans took further political aim at the Clintons, as Bernstein (2016: 11) comments:

> The Republican right has always looked at the Clintons as radical leftist demons – exemplars of the ultra-liberalism

the right despises, even though Bill and Hillary were more conventional centre-left in their politics. Hardly radicals. And their enemies became even more enraged after Bill survived impeachment and Hillary went on to the Senate and then candidate for president. The Clinton presidential legacy, in tatters after impeachment was redeemed after its enemies had thought 'Clintonism' was dead. Redeemed largely by Hillary.

Hillary Clinton's political career

Hillary Clinton really began to take her own political prospects seriously only when she was approached in 1998 by New York officials about running for Daniel Patrick Moynihan's Senate seat. As Traister (2016) comments, the timing was not good, as Moynihan had announced his retirement a month before the vote on Bill Clinton's impeachment. Hillary had spent two terms in the White House and was not sure that she wanted to plunge into a senatorial position immediately. As Traister (2016) comments:

> She had good reason to be scared. By 1999, even without having pursued her own political path, Clinton had learned what it might entail to be a woman who competed. She had taken her husband's last name after his 1980 re-election defeat in Arkansas had been blamed on her independence; she'd done cookie bake off penance for her remarks about prioritizing career over domesticity; everything from her friend Vince Foster's death to the wandering attentions of her husband had been tied to her purported ruthlessness.

Senatorial race

Bernstein (2016: 13) says that the decision on the Senate race in New York State was about 'redemption': 'So she ran for the Senate seeking redemption, redemption of their political journey together, redemption of all the good things that happened during the Clinton presidency.' In her interview with Traister (2016), Clinton was asked how she saw the issue of competition and how women are seen in this regard. Traister asked Clinton how she defined this: 'Did she mean men's fears that ambitious women would take up space that used to belong exclusively to them?' Clinton responded "One hundred percent", nodding forcefully. Clinton gave an example of a situation at Harvard that highlights this. She and a friend from Wellesley were sitting for the Law School Admission Test at Harvard.

> "We were in this huge cavernous room", she said, "hundreds of people were taking this test, and there weren't many women there. This friend and I were waiting for the test to begin and the young men around us were like, 'What do you think [you're] doing? How dare you take a spot from one of us?' It was just a relentless harangue". Clinton and her friend were stunned. They'd spent four years at a women's college, where these kinds of gender dynamics didn't apply. "I remember one young man said, 'If you get into law school and I don't and I have to go to Vietnam and get killed, it's your fault.'" (Traister, 2016)

As Clinton went on to say to Traister: "'So yeah, … that level of visceral … fear, anxiety, insecurity plays a role" in how America regards ambitious women.' In terms of being on the campaign trail, this is how Clinton defines that sexism: "'The sexism is less virulent now than it was in 2008", she said but she still encounters people on rope lines who tell her: 'I really admire you, I really like you, I just don't know if I can vote for a woman to be president'. "I mean they come to my events and then they say that to me".'

Bernstein (2016: 14) comments that while she was not a distinguished politician in terms of important legislation, she was successful in working across the aisle. She started doing the preparatory work for a future run at the presidency. She became a member of the Armed Services Committee, to bolster her qualifications. She was also aware that if she voted against the Iraq War, it might make her path to the presidency more difficult.

Clinton as Secretary of State

Clinton saw her appointment as Secretary of State as a valuable opportunity to do important work that she was qualified to do. She would also be in the forefront of the international imagination. Bernstein (2016: 15) notes, however, that she was disappointed in the role:

> She expected as secretary of state to be a real policy maker who would help shape President Obama's foreign and national security policies. It turns out she was shut out of real policy making and from having great influence on

the president. So she became an ambassador at large to the world … And the goodwill that she generated around the world for both this country and for President Obama's policies was extraordinary.

Clinton, in the words of the inimitable MSNBC, was a 'policy wonk' and she had a mastery of the minutiae of policy issues. However, there is sexism in how she was viewed in this regard. Traister (2016) relates how Joe Scarborough from MSNBC's *Morning Joe* commented on it: "'You want to go to sleep tonight? Go to Hillary Clinton's website and start reading policy positions'". As Traister (2016) comments,

> It is not uncommon for women to be tagged as dull pragmatists in this way. The history of politics and of progressive movements, after all, is one of women doing the drudge work and men giving the inspiring speeches. It wasn't Dorothy Height or Rosa Parks or Pauli Murray or Diane Nash or Anna Hedgeman – hardworking activists and lawyers and organizers – who gave big speeches on the steps of the Lincoln Memorial.

There is little doubt that despite significant skills and knowledge that would have made her a powerful leader, Clinton did not run a good presidential campaign; and, as Traister (2016) comments, for inspiration in presidential campaigns we still demand 'the rhetorical high notes'. It was clear that during the campaign Clinton simply did not reach those high notes. She has of course reached those high notes many times before, especially in her speeches on 'women's rights are human rights' and in her 2008 concession speech when she talked about the '18 million cracks in the glass ceiling'.

Symbolism, feminism and the press

The ongoing criticism of Clinton is that she has failed to use the symbolic power of her position to best advantage. Her view is that symbolic power is not going to effect real change, although she does admit that she is now more embracing of it. She is a results-oriented person but sometimes loses the significance of charisma in this process. There is also an ambivalence about her role in the world and the lack of privacy that brings, borne out of defensiveness and experience. She has, after all, been in the front line defending her family against the attacks made as a result of Bill Clinton's multiple infidelities. As

Traister (2016) comments, 'A lifetime spent in the searing spotlight has taught her that exposure too often equals evisceration. It's worth remembering that Clinton's public identity was shaped during the feminist backlash of the '80s and early '90s when saying that you didn't want to bake cookies was enough to start a culture war.'

In addition, Clinton hates the press and does not ride on the same plane with them, as other candidates do; and many of the press corps are novices with little or no history or experience of candidates and campaigns. As Traister (2016) comments:

> Most of the travelling reporters are too young to remember the way Clinton was barbecued by the media from the beginning, labelled too radical, too feminist, too independent, too influential; dangerously conniving, ugly and unfuckable. But it's clear that even today she and her campaign feel that they can't win with the press, that the storylines about her are already written.

There is little doubt that Clinton is a bad campaigner and, after her experiences, it is hardly surprising that she does not like the press and is 'skittish', years later, about being called 'a left-wing feminazi'. Her bad relationship with the press means that she is never cut any slack, as Traister (2016) writes: 'Clinton pays for not having a warmer, closer relationship with reporters. She does not enjoy the goodwill that someone like Joe Biden – a king of mis-statements, prone to offending entire nationalities – has earned, which permits him to get out of jail-time again and again.'

Clinton is clearly repulsed by Trump, but the US has to learn from its mistakes and accept a period of international relations where it suffers from the folly of electing his. Whether it ends in impeachment or resignation or other, only time will tell; but the key thing for the US is to look beyond Trump. As Traister (2016) comments, in voting for Trump, the country knew what it was getting: 'Trump does away with any pretext. He calls women pieces of ass and rates them on scales one to ten; he encourages violence, fails to firmly disavow David Duke, promises walls to keep out immigrants and to ban Muslims from entering the country.'

Gender and the failure of the Hillary Clinton campaign

It is very clear that gender did play a part in the election defeat of Hillary Clinton. As Traister (2016) comments, 'It is one of the factors that shaped Hillary Clinton and it is one of the factors that shapes how we respond to her. Whatever your feelings about Clinton herself, this election raises important questions about how we define leadership in this country, how we feel about women who try to claim it, flawed though it might be.'

In a less philosophical but more political analysis of the election failure, Molly Ball (2016), writing in *The Atlantic* on 'Why Hillary Clinton Lost', relates the failures to a poor campaign strategy, the ceding of the white, male working-class vote, the failure to relate to minorities and the young. However, the failure to tap into the 'Obama coalition' cannot fully be laid at Clinton's door, as Cornell Belcher, the political commentator notes, as this latter group were never solid supporters of the Democrats. These were Obama's voters rather than Democratic voters. Clinton arrogantly assumed that the Obama coalition would support her – this was a mistake; and that in addition she could target Republican women – not realizing that these were not educated, professional women who had slipped into a right-wing populist mode, and that as Traister (2016) reporting on Joe Dinkin of the Working Families Party comments, '"being a republican voter means already having come to terms with voting for disgusting racists and sexists some times"'.

Ball (2016) also points out the failure of the Clinton campaign to focus on a strong economic message, but relying on a 'soft' social message was also a failure of the campaign. Her perspective that 'America is already great', and therefore ignoring the white and black working-class who were hurting, was folly. She also misjudged the general critique of Trump by focusing on his personality, sexism and racism, which were already 'baked into' the support, and failed to focus on his wealth and how this made him unable to understand the lives of working Americans. It allowed Trump to put on the little red hat and claim he was the candidate of working America.

The campaign trail is a brutal one and, despite the fact that Trump is older, overweight and a clear candidate for a stroke, he was a street fighter on the campaign trail and fought for every vote. Clinton held fewer events than Trump and appeared to be taking winning for granted.

The result was not a resounding defeat for Hillary Clinton, and she won the popular vote, but it highlighted the need for a Democratic Party and candidate that recognizes what has happened to American society. As Traister (2016) comments of the US electorate and society:

> if, as in this election, a man who spews hate and vulgarity,
> with no comprehension of how government works can

become presidentially plausible because he is magnetic while a capable, workaholic woman who knows policy inside out struggles because she is not magnetic, perhaps we should reevaluate … It's worth asking to what degree charisma, as we have defined it, is a masculine trait. Can a woman appeal to the country in the same way we are used to men doing it?

Conclusion

This final chapter has reflected on the kinds of obstacles and prejudices that women public intellectuals have always confronted within academia and in political life. They have faced criticism from other feminists, through to abuse from presidential candidates like Trump. The final two chapters of the book have considered examples of contemporary women public intellectuals who have made it to the top in academic and political terms. The calibre, quality and sheer determination of these women has been considered. The idea that we should disregard these successful women in the US and not see them as role models because they constitute 'elite middle-class women' and thus are unrepresentative is an absurd proposition. These women have not made it to the top because of wealth or significant connections; they have made it to the top through being highly intelligent, but also through hard work, grit and commitment. The structure of university education in the US provides for women to take these opportunities and serve in different administrations, while afterwards returning to academic positions, should they want to. The UK and other countries have much to learn from the US in this regard. This book has shown that across the centuries and the decades women have emerged as significant public intellectuals. We can look forward to a positive future of success for women, politics and the public sphere if the lives of the women outlined in the chapters of this book are typical of how we measure success.

Conclusion

Women, Politics and the Public Sphere has explored the relationship between women, political discourse and political representation historically, contemporaneously and cross-culturally. In the chapters of this book I have traced the emergence of women public intellectuals from the 18th century to the present day.

Chapter One outlined the significance of the bluestockings, bluestocking circles and bluestocking philosophy and showed how the gender politics of the bluestockings can be differentiated from the radical politics of women political thinkers and philosophers such as Mary Wollstonecraft and Catherine Macaulay. As Kelly (2001) notes, the conservative gender politics of the bluestockings is in stark contrast to the republicanism of Catherine Macaulay and the gender-equality rhetoric of Mary Wollstonecraft. Kelly goes further in describing the 'counter-Revolutionary' conservatism of the bluestockings as part of a 'remasculinization' of culture.

However, despite their divergent views, emphasis was given by both groups to women's education and to building up networking and mentoring of women. They established the basis of the emergence of women as public intellectuals. These women were prolific in their publications and social engagement in establishing women's scholarship.

Secondly, Elizabeth Montagu acted as a mentor for women writers and used her house as a meeting place for bluestocking circles. The focus of the circles was women, although some men did attend. Eger (2005) notes that Montagu's circles encouraged debate and dialogue between men and women in periodicals and literature. Thirdly, members of the bluestockings also established women as significant scholarly authors, including Elizabeth Montagu and Elizabeth Carter. As Eger (2005) notes, Montagu also encouraged women from a diversity of backgrounds to move into publishing. Fourthly, the bluestockings also established a strong sense of community between women. However, Guest (2003) notes that they did not have a distinctly political character, unlike men's association with the world of letters, which gave them a more distinctively political character.

What is clear is that the bluestockings, among others, provided the potential for the growth and expansion of women as public intellectuals in Britain and Europe. Hesse's (2005a) work on Europe shows the expansion of women as public intellectuals in a range of institutions in society and, increasingly, into the professions. Montagu also had connections in Europe with the French salonnières and in her collections of letters with other members of the bluestockings. Kelly (2015) notes that women public intellectuals began to expand to include less elite women and more middle-class women.

There was inevitably a backlash against these women public intellectuals, and Eger (2008) shows that this occurred in the 19th century. However, the intellectual climate for women as a result of the bluestockings did inspire a number of radical thinkers who emerged alongside and subsequently.

In Chapter Two, the concept of the public sphere was explored, drawing on Habermas's conceptualization of the public sphere. Guest (2003) draws on Habermas to explain the gendered character of the public sphere in the 18th century. She shows that the underpinning of the bourgeois public sphere by the development of the educated classes helps to explain and understand how the bluestockings created the opportunity of a female political voice.

It also opened up the ability of more explicitly political writers such as Wollstonecraft and Macaulay to express a more explicitly political view. The responses of different feminist thinkers and writers to Habermas's model have been varied, and some are critical of the hegemonic character of the model. Guest (2003) makes the point that in the Habermasian model women can be involved in public and political affairs if they are linked to notions of propriety and patriotism. Some writers see the growth of bluestocking circles as bridging the public and private divide.

As was shown in Chapter Two, Habermas's view of the public sphere is a gendered one. His attitude to women in the public sphere is ambiguous and he did not see women as making a significant contribution to opinions emerging within the public sphere. His views are challenged by Eger (2001), among others. She criticizes his model of the growth of the public sphere, which sees professional and commercial middle-class men as dominating political and social discourse. A number of feminist writers show how women were also highly visible in the public sphere in terms of their political and personal lives and their work as writers and editors of journals. Eger (2001) also shows how a number of women writers lived on their literary earnings and were independent economically. Writers such as Macaulay also produced prestigious works that were recognized internationally. This makes Habermas's view of women's role in the public sphere problematic.

As I noted in Chapter Two, what Habermas's work does do is to highlight the changing class nature of public intellectuals. The aristocratic and wealthy character of the bluestockings was expanded into a broader conceptualization of the professional class, and women were seen to be actively involved in a range of literary and other spheres of work such as publishing and printing, illustrating and librarianship. The contribution of Habermas's analysis of the public sphere is to show indirectly how women were involved in an expanding education and print culture that fundamentally supported the expansion of a public intelligentsia. Kelly (2001) sees this period as a watershed and the bluestockings as remodelling intellectual culture so that women could gain greater participation.

Fleming (2013) shows that despite the limitations in Habermas's work, feminists can draw on his distinctions between the public and the private. These issues are particularly relevant in the analysis of contemporary women public intellectuals as outlined in the final chapters of the book. Fraser (1990) also challenges Habermas's hegemonic view of the public sphere and claims that his focus on the liberal public sphere, while ignoring other public spheres, makes his assessment of the public sphere inadequate. Of course Habermas is venerated by a tradition of male-dominated social theorists but, as I showed in Chapter Two, a wide range of feminist theorists challenge his model in a significant way. I also extended the debate on liberalism, justice and feminism through the work of Nussbaum (1999, 2013) and Pateman (1988, 1989) and showed that Habermas's focus on the liberal public sphere aligns with a model that is about the dominance of men and the subordination of women.

Kelly (2015) shows that the expansion of bluestockings into a broader range of public intellectuals clearly shows that women were making inroads into a wider range of professions. Kelly also shows that the concept of public intellectual was beginning to emerge only slowly and began to apply to women only in the 1820s and 1830s.

In Chapter Three, two of the foremost women public intellectuals, Catherine Macaulay and Mary Wollstonecraft, were explored. Their writing and political commentary provide different models of voice and advocacy for women, and both offer significant contributions to political discourse around women's political rights in the late 18th century. Their work advanced the role and position of women public intellectuals and reflects the monumental upheavals caused by both the American Declaration of Independence in 1776 and the French Revolution in 1789. Both are described as women in a man's world and as prominent republican thinkers. Guest (2003) maintains that by the 1790s Catherine Macaulay and Mary Wollstonecraft had created a level of 'political articulacy' and 'public audibility' that contribute to modern feminist politics in Britain.

Macaulay was well established internationally as a result of her eight-volume *History* long before Wollstonecraft published *A Vindication of the Rights of Woman* (1792). One of the key contributions of the political discourse within Wollstonecraft's text was the challenge of the position of women in society and the relations between men and women. Wollstonecraft wrote more directly about the position of women in society. Macaulay was interested as a republican in full male suffrage but did not address the question of women's suffrage. In fact, neither Wollstonecraft nor Macaulay was supportive of full suffrage for women, and neither believed that working-class women had sufficient capacity for suffrage. As Hill (1995) shows, this was not untypical of how 18th-century radicals understood women's rights.

The writings of Wollstonecraft and Macaulay on women and education put the emphasis on education, leading to greater independence for women. Wollstonecraft went further in arguing that women should also work. Many see Wollstonecraft as an early feminist and as going beyond radical politics to sexual liberation for women. The private lives of both women became the subject of public criticism for their relationships or marriages with younger men, and in Wollstonecraft's case for having children out of wedlock.

Wollstonecraft was an important advocate for professional and middle-class women and, more broadly, as Kelly (1992, 2015) shows, for a process of modernization. More particularly she was one of a new breed of women public intellectuals who supported herself by 'literary intellectual work'. Kelly also shows that Wollstonecraft challenged male-dominated discourses such as historiography and philosophy and this established women as more fully public intellectuals in their own right and as an example of modernization. Caine (1997) maintains that Wollstonecraft's *Vindication of the Rights of Woman* is a founding text of Anglo-American feminism and that her novel *Maria* shows how Wollstonecraft was disillusioned by how the French Revolution responded to women and democracy. Wollstonecraft, more so than Macaulay, attempted to bridge the public and the private by arguing that aspects of good citizenship included being a mother.

Wollstonecraft attempted to transpose the 'inalienable rights of men' from the French and American Revolutions to include women's rights. Gunther-Canada (1996) makes the important point that Wollstonecraft's two *Vindications* were important early feminist documents because they focus on the problematic nature of political discourse that excludes women's rights. Gunther-Canada (1996) also shows how Wollstonecraft demonstrated her understanding of political theory and her challenge to patriarchal politics.

As I noted in Chapter Three, Wollstonecraft was very contemporary in her thinking, extending the claims of Enlightenment humanism to women and establishing a relationship between sex and citizenship, and she also establishes herself as a woman writing about the political rights of women. She was also critical of women for allowing that capacity for reason to be side-tracked by vanity and idle pleasures, but she saw education as centrally important in this regard. She saw women's capacity for citizenship changing over time through education. She viewed women as moving into many areas of the professions and she showed that to achieve this women must redefine their responsibilities away from the domestic sphere. Wollstonecraft's political views were challenged by right-wing thinkers after details of her personal life were revealed by her husband, William Godwin.

Catherine Macaulay shares many of Wollstonecraft's political aspirations and, given her intellectual contribution, can be seen as advancing the position of women as public intellectuals. In Macaulay's case the driving force was republicanism, as opposed to feminism. O'Brien (2005) comments that while Macaulay's writings offer a significant contribution to politics, they do not reflect on the 'historical progress of women'; however, O'Brien notes, methodologically, in her writing, Macaulay made a contribution as a feminist historian. As with Wollstonecraft, Macaulay challenged conventional norms in both her politics and her private life.

While Macaulay's most influential book is her eight-volume *History of England* (1763–83), her most important work addressing women's issues was *Letters on Education* (1790). Hill (1992) also shows that her commentary on women was influenced by her personal experiences. Interestingly, Wollstonecraft reviewed Macaulay's book for a leading journal of the time. Gunther-Canada (2003) makes an important point in commenting that by linking co-education to civic education Macaulay and Wollstonecraft link education with the enfranchisement of women as citizens. Gunther-Canada (2003) also says that Macaulay champions intellectual equality in the *Letters* and is critical of mechanisms that hold women back, but she is critical of Macaulay's focus on wealthy women and on elite, home-based education.

By comparison, Wollstonecraft's views on education were transformative. She is more radical than Macaulay in challenging laws that discriminate against women, separating them into public and private spheres. Macaulay never raised the issue of women's suffrage. Gunther-Canada (2003) shows how Wollstonecraft went beyond Macaulay in that while Macaulay demanded intellectual equality, Wollstonecraft called for political equality. There is little doubt that

Macaulay's work had a significant influence on Wollstonecraft. While these important public intellectuals never met, they corresponded and shared published work.

As with many women who are public intellectuals, both Wollstonecraft and Macaulay suffered abuse from right-wing commentary, and this has of course remained the case, as is shown in the analysis of women public intellectuals who have held office in contemporary US politics. Both Wollstonecraft and Macaulay suffered vicious satire and abuse from literary figures of the time. Much of the criticism also came from conservative women within the bluestockings. Both women were the target of moralistic and sexist commentary on account of their relationships with and marriages to younger men.

Chapter Four showed how changing attitudes towards women writers and thinkers as public intellectuals during the 18th century and beyond were encouraged by the expansion of print culture as women became more involved in the world of ideas and publishing. Hesse (2005a) notes that in France the number of women writers in print increased to over 300 during the period of revolution, while in Italy and France the number of academies and learned societies showed a significant increase in the number of women. A range of women public intellectuals emerged as significant writers on a wide range of subjects both within and outside the bluestockings.

Kelly (2001) makes the important point that the bluestockings transformed from being 'learned ladies' to 'cosmopolitan intellectuals', and he frames the change in terms of a remodelling of intellectual culture, with women playing a more significant role. This had already been marked by the work of Elizabeth Carter and Elizabeth Montagu. Despite this, women were still limited in terms of their ability to contribute fully to public discourse. However, the link between the professionalization of writing and the emergence of a new middle class established a broader basis for women's participation.

Women's voices were increasingly influential in public opinion. One of the major journals of the time, *The Female Spectator*, gave voice on a wide range of subjects and encouraged a wider readership among women. In addition, and as was shown in Chapter Three, both Macaulay and Wollstonecraft contributed to the professionalization of women as public intellectuals. Wollstonecraft in particular put the emphasis on the development of critical and reflexive thought in women so that they could develop a national identity for a modern nation-state. Kelly (2015) shows how Wollstonecraft was innovative in its methodology and in its challenges to 'the Old Order'.

Kelly also shows how Wollstonecraft's later work opposed the rejection of modernization, which many had argued as a result of the anarchy coming from the French Revolution. However, Caine (1997) shows that Wollstonecraft was despondent about the emancipatory potential for women of the French Revolution. As Chapter Four showed, Wollstonecraft was an immensely gifted social commentator, combining a theory of women's rights with a wider critique of social transformation within the French Revolution. Similarly Macaulay was an immensely influential social commentator and a profoundly critical historian. Her work, as noted, was recognized by significant figures in North America, including Benjamin Franklin, and both Wollstonecraft and Macaulay provided an opening up of literary, methodological, political and social discourses.

Chapter Four also indicated how the 19th century showed the emergence of American and British women writers, commentators and thinkers. The key form of social commentary within British writers was the novel, and writers such as Virginia Woolf have provided important examples of women public intellectuals. Eger (2008) makes the important point in showing the succession of the novel from the bluestockings to the 19th century. Writers such as Jane Austen had used the novel to great effect as a form of social commentary.

The bluestockings as a group provided an important framework for the emergence of groups such as the Bloomsbury Group, which included significant women public intellectuals such as Virginia Woolf and Vanessa Bell. Marcus (2000) shows how Virginia Woolf provided an important contribution as both a woman and a feminist public intellectual, with contributions to 'literary feminist politics'. Marcus makes some important broader linkages in this regard with 'feminist anger or radicalism', 'feminist use of androgyny' as a concept, for the 'relationship of socialism to feminism', 'feminism to pacifism' and 'patriarchy and fascism'.

While women public intellectuals had not formed a critical mass by the 19th century, the growth of universities and women's access to a university education provided for the emergence of the 'New Woman', and subsequently for the growth of social movements accelerating the movement of women public intellectuals into the public domain.

Chapter Five looked at the growth of social movements as an important factor in the emergence of women public intellectuals, and additionally the movement of women more fully into the political sphere. There is some divergence by feminist historians and writers on how significant the suffrage movement was in relation to the history of women's politics. Vickery (2001) argues that the suffrage movement was the starting point historically of women in politics. However, Cowman (2010) makes the point that this implies that there was no history on women in politics before the suffrage movement. There is detailed and significant information on women's involvement in politics prior to the suffrage movement, and there is ample evidence, as I show, of women's involvement in all aspects of political life. Caine (1997) maintains that it was the advocacy of political rights in the French Revolution that in fact marked the 'birth of modern feminism'.

The chapter focused on a number of different historians on the role that women played in politics from the 18th century onwards and showed that aristocratic women wielded considerable power politically, even though they did not hold political office directly.

In addition, the growth of print culture meant that women could organize political pamphlets, and the rapid expansion of coffee-houses provided a venue for debate.

Cowman shows how women were involved in a range of political movements before the suffrage movement, including the anti-slavery movement, which attracted women from across the social classes.

The 19th century saw a range of small and larger groupings of women who were politically active. This was accompanied by the growth of journals such as the *English Woman's Journal*, which acted as a campaigning tool as well as a periodical. This brought together a wider range of women and focused on expanding the employment of women and expanding the opportunities for women in higher education.

In addition, there was an expansion of higher education, including the founding of Girton College in Cambridge, with women increasingly moving into the professions. The growth of these different dimensions led to what Rendall (1985) calls 'a cautious liberal-feminist politics' that set the tone for the emergence of the women's movement. By the mid-19th century women were focusing on issues of relevance to women's social and political position, particularly married women's property rights. Another dimension of women's political engagement was philanthropic work, which provided a further opportunity for women to become politically active, although Hollis (1987) said that this did little to increase women's parliamentary suffrage. By the middle of the 19th century the political party system was beginning to emerge, but women had no part to play as they were not recognized as party members. This changed only in 1892, with the birth of the Labour Party.

The growth of the women's movement can be traced back to the suffrage movement, which began to emerge from 1897. The suffrage movement was specifically directed to securing the vote for women. Cowman shows how the emergence of the 'New Woman' coincided with the suffrage movement and young, educated women who were fearless in the face of male-dominated politics. However, Lawrence (2001) notes that political meetings were characterized by violence from men towards women as they saw women as becoming increasingly visible at political meetings. Women's suffrage dominated the first half of the 20th century and historians have maintained that the inter-war period was characterized by a lull in feminist politics. However, feminist historians have argued that feminist groupings were active between the 1940s and 1950s.

The growth of the women's movement and the emergence of feminism and the women's liberation movement (WLM) have been extensively documented and have not been the focus of this book directly, other than to recognize the historical and transformative impact they had on women globally. Both the WLM and the growth of feminism produced a critical mass of women public intellectuals that transformed the social and political landscape for women (and men). As Cowman (2010) shows, the changing landscape provided the backdrop for women to move into party politics and to demand greater representation of women in politics.

The last two chapters of the book focused on contemporary women public intellectuals in the US who have served in different political administrations. I chose to focus on the US because these women represent a profile of women public intellectuals who have moved from being highly successful academics in top universities in the US, into important political positions in Republican and Democratic administrations. Beyond this, the reason for their selection was because they have made a significant contribution through the roles they have played in policy formulation in different administrations.

There are of course successful women public intellectuals in Europe, the UK and other parts of the world; however, very few countries show the same profile of success in gender politics that the US does, and the public intellectuals outlined here have profiles that stands independently of the administrations they served. Many of these women could easily have stood for election as president in the US; Hillary Clinton, of course, did stand. Many wanted Condoleezza Rice to run as president; Elizabeth Warren may yet run in the 2020 election. In other cases Susan Rice may stand for the Senate. The contemporary women public intellectuals profiled in this book offer outstanding models of women public intellectuals, but there is still much more to achieve.

References

Adams, H. (1799) *Summary History of New England: from the first settlement at Plymouth to the acceptance of the federal Constitution*. Dedham, MA: H. Mann and H. Adams.

Amos, V. and Parmar, P. (1984) 'Challenging Imperial Feminism', *Feminist Review*, 17(1): 3–19.

Ball, M. (2016) 'Why Hillary Clinton Lost', *The Atlantic*, 15 November, www.theatlantic.com

Bell, K. (2010) 'Life's Work: Condoleezza Rice, 66th Secretary of State', *Harvard Business Review*, Jan–Feb, www.hrb.org

Bernstein, C. (2007) *A Woman in Charge: The Life of Hillary Rodham Clinton*. London/New York: Hutchinson.

Bernstein, C. (2016) 'Who is Hillary Clinton?', http://edition.cnn.com

Bodichon, B. (1854) *A Brief Summary of the Laws of England Concerning Women, Together with a Few Observations Thereon*. London: John Chapman. Reprinted in S. Bell and K. Offen (eds) (1983) *Women, Family and Freedom: The Debate in Documents, Vol 1, 1750–1880*. Stanford, CA: Stanford University Press.

Bothwell, E. (2018) 'Female Leadership Moves Backwards in World's Top Universities', *Times Higher Education*, 8 March, www.timeshighereducation.com

Brooks, A. (1997) *Postfeminism: Feminism, Cultural Theory and Cultural Forms*. London/New York: Routledge.

Brooks, A. (2008) 'Reconceptualising Reflexivity and Dissonance in Professional and Personal Domains', *British Journal of Sociology* 59(3): 539–59.

Brooks, A. (2014) '"The Affective Turn" in the Social Sciences and the Gendered Nature of Emotions: Theorizing Emotions in the Social Sciences from 1800 to the Present', in D. Lemmings and A. Brooks (eds) *Emotions and Social Change: Historical and Sociological Perspectives*. London/New York: Routledge: 43–62.

Brooks, A. and Wee, L. (2008) 'Reflexivity and the Transformation of Gender Identity: Reviewing the Potential for Change in a Cosmopolitan City', *Sociology*, 42(3): 503–21.

Brooks, A. and Wee, L. (2012) 'Negotiating Gendered Subjectivity in Enterprise Culture: Metaphor and Entrepreneurial Discourses', *Gender, Work and Organization* 19(6): 573–91.

Brown, J.H. (2008) '10 Percent Intellectual: the Mind of Condoleezza Rice', *The Centre for Media Democracy*, *PR Watch*, 21 May.

Bruenig, E. (2015) 'Sheryl Sandberg's Lean In Philosophy Doesn't Just Ignore Disadvantaged Women, It Hurts Their Cause', *New Republic*, 9 March, www.newrepublic.com

Bumiller, E. (2007) *Condoleezza Rice: An American Life*. New York: Random House.

Burney, F. (1768 [1982]) *Evelina. Or the History of a Young Lady's Entrance into the World*, (eds) E.A. Bloom and L.D. Bloom. London: Penguin Classics.

Burney, F. (1782 [2009]) *Cecilia or Memoirs of an Heiress. By the Author of Evelina*. New York: Oxford World Classics.

Burney, F. (1796 [1999]) *Camilla or a Picture of Youth. By the Author of Evelina and Cecilia*. New York: Oxford World Classics.

Burney, F. (1832) *Memoirs of Doctor Burney, Arranged from Manuscripts, from Family Papers, and from Personal Collections*, 3 vols. London.

Caine, B. (1997) *English Feminism, 1780–1980*. Oxford: Oxford University Press.

Carter, E. (1758) (trans) *All the Works of Epictetus, which are Now Extant*. London.

Carter, E. (1809) *A series of letters between Mrs Elizabeth Carter and Miss Catherine Talbot from 1741 to 1770. To which are added letters from Mrs Elizabeth Carer to Mrs Vesey, between 1763 and 1787*. London: Rivington.

Chapone, H. (1773) *Letters on the Improvement of the Mind, Addressed to a Young Lady. In Two Volumes by Mrs Chapone*. London.

Clinton, H. (2017) *What Happened?*, New York: Simon and Schuster.

Colley, L. (1992) *Britons: Forging the Nation, 1707–1837*. London.

Cowman, K. (2010) *Women in British Politics c 1689–1979*. Basingstoke: Palgrave, Macmillan.

Crawford, P. and Gowing, L. (2000) *Women's Worlds in Seventeenth Century England: A Sourcebook*. London: Routledge.

Davidoff, L. and Hall, C. (1987) *Family Fortunes: Men and Women of the English Middle Class, 1780–1850*. Chicago: Chicago University Press.

Desai, A. (1993) 'Introduction', in Mary Wortley Montagu, *Turkish Embassy Letters*. London: William and Chato.

Dowd, M. (2013) 'Pompom Girl for Feminism', *The New York Times*, 23 February, www.nytimes.com

Drezner, D. (2008) '*Twice as Good: Condoleezza Rice and Her Path to Power*; *Condoleezza Rice: An American Life*; *The Confidante: Condoleezza Rice and the Creation of the Bush Legacy* by Marcus Mabry, Elisabeth Bumiller, Glenn Kessler', Review in *Foreign Affairs*, Nov–Dec, www.foreignaffairs.com

Eger, E. (2001) 'Representing Culture; "The Nine Living Muses of Great Britain" (1779)', in E. Eger, C. Grant, C. O'Gallchoir and P. Warburton (eds) *Women, Writing and the Public Sphere 1700–1830*. Cambridge: Cambridge University Press: 104–32.

Eger, E. (2005) 'The Noblest Commerce of Mankind: Conversation and Community in the Bluestocking Circle', in S. Knott and B. Taylor (eds) *Women, Gender and Enlightenment*. Basingstoke/New York: Palgrave, Macmillan: 288–306.

Eger, E. (2008) 'The Bluestocking Legacy' in E. Eger and L. Peltz *Brilliant Women: 18th-century Bluestockings*. London: National Portrait Gallery: 126–52.

Eger, E. and Peltz, L. (2008) *Brilliant Women: 18th-century Bluestockings*. London: National Portrait Gallery.

Eger, E., Grant, G., Gallchoir, C.O. and Warburton, P. (eds) (2001) *Women, Writing and the Public Sphere*. Cambridge: Cambridge University Press.

Fleming, M. (2013) 'Women and the "Public Use of Reason"', in J. Meehan (ed) *Feminists Read Habermas: Gendering the Subject of Discourse*. London/New York: Routledge: 117–39.

Foran, C. (2017) 'A Triumphant Moment for Elizabeth Warren', *The Atlantic*, 8 February, www.theatlantic.com

Foreman, A. (1997 [2001]) 'A Politician's Politician: Georgina, Duchess of Devonshire and the Whig Party', in E. Chalus and H. Barker (eds) *Gender in Eighteenth Century England: Roles, Representations and Responsibilities*. London: Addison Wesley Longman: 179–205.

Foster, D. (2016a) 'Sheryl Sandberg and Christiane Lagarde Have Done Nothing to Advance Feminism', *Guardian*, 2 February, www.theguardian.com

Foster, D. (2016b) *Lean Out*. London: Duncan Baird Publishers.

Fraser, N. (1990) 'Rethinking the Public Sphere: A Contribution to the Critique of Actually Existing Democracy', *Social Text*, 25–26: 56–80.

Fraser, N. (1995) 'What's Critical about Critical Theory', in J. Meehan (ed) *Feminists Read Habermas: Gendering the Subject of Discourse*. London/New York: Routledge: 21–55.

Frazer, E. (2011) 'Mary Wollstonecraft and Catherine Macaulay on Education', *Oxford Review of Education*, 37 (5): 603–17.

Freedland, J. (2007) 'Madame Secretary', *The New York Times*, 1 July, www.nytimes.com

Garber, M. (2017) '"Nevertheless She Persisted" and the Age of the Weaponised Meme', *The Atlantic*, 8 February, www.theatlantic.com

Glasser, S.B. (2017) 'Condi Rice on Trump: "Words Do Matter"', *Politico Magazine*, 15 May, www.politico.com/magazine/story/2017/05/15/condoleezza-rice-thefull-transcript-215133

Godwin, W. (1798 [1987]) *Memoirs of the Author of a Vindication on the Rights of Woman*. Harmondsworth: Penguin Books.

Goldberg, J. (2017) '"The Autocratic Element": Can America Ever Recover from the Trump Administration', *The Atlantic*, October, www.theatlantic.com

Gonda, E. (2001) 'Misses, Murderesses and Magdalens: Women in the Public Eye' in E. Eger, C. Grant, C. O'Gallchoir and P. Warburton (eds) *Women, Writing and the Public Sphere, 1700–1830*. Cambridge: Cambridge University Press: 53–75.

Goodman, D. (1995a) 'Suzanne Necker's Melanges: Gender, writing and publicity' in D. Goodman and E.C. Goldsmith (eds) *Going Public: Women and Publishing in Early Modern France*. Ithaca, NY: Cornell University Press.

Goodman, D. (1995b) 'Introduction' in D. Goodman and E.C. Goldsmith (eds) *Going Public: Women and Publishing in Early Modern France*. Ithaca, NY: Cornell University Press.

Graham, D.A. (2017a) 'Did Susan Rice Do Anything Wrong by Asking to 'Unmask' Trump Officials?', *The Atlantic*, 3 April, www.theatlantic.com

Graham, D.A. (2017b) 'Why Won't Susan Rice Testify to Congress?', *The Atlantic*, 4 May, www.theatlantic.com

Green, E. (2017) 'After 2016's Losses, Elizabeth Warren tells Democrats: "Shame on Us"', *The Washington Post*, 18 April, www.washingtonpost.com

Guest, H. (2003) 'Bluestocking Feminism', in N. Pohl and B.A. Schellenberg (eds) *Reconsidering the Bluestockings*. San Marino, CA.: Huntington Library: 59–81.

Guest, H. (2005) 'Women, Liberty and the Nation', in S. Knott and B. Taylor (eds) *Women, Gender and Enlightenment*. Basingstoke: Palgrave, Macmillan: 519–23.

Gunther-Canada, W. (1996) 'Mary Wollstonecraft's "Wild Wish": Confounding Sex in the Discourse of Political Rights', in M.J. Falco (ed) *Feminist Interpretations of Mary Wollstonecraft*. Philadelphia: Pennsylvania State University Press.

Gunther-Canada, W. (2003) 'Cultivating Virtue: Catherine Macaulay and Mary Wollstonecraft on Civic Education', *Women and Politics*, 25(3): 47–70.

Habermas, J. (1989) *The Structural Transformation of the Public Sphere: An Inquiry into a Category of Bourgeois Society*. Cambridge: Cambridge University Press.

Halsband, R. (1956) *The Life of Mary Wortley Montagu*. Oxford: Clarendon Press.

Harris, P. (2012) 'Susan Rice: the Sharp UN Ambassador Fighting for her Political Future', *Guardian*, 30 November, www.theguardian.com

Haywood, E. (1744) *The Female Spectator*. London: H. Gardner.

Heller, D. (1998) 'Bluestocking Salons and the Public Sphere', *Eighteenth-Century Life* 22: 59–82.

Heller, D. (ed) (2015) *Bluestockings Now: The Evolution of a Social Role*. Farnham: Ashgate.

Hess, A. (2013) 'Lean Where?', *Slate*, 8 March, www.slate.com

Hesse, C. (2005) 'Women Intellectuals in the Enlightened Republic of Letters', in S. Knott and B. Taylor (eds) *Women, Gender and Enlightenment*. Basingstoke/New York: Palgrave, Macmillan: 259–65.

Hill, B. (1992) *The Republican Virago: The Life and Times of Catherine Macaulay*. Oxford: Clarendon Press.

Hill, B. (1995) The Links Between Mary Wollstonecraft and Catherine Macaulay: New Evidence, *Women's History Review*, 4 (2): 177–92.

Hollis, P. (1987) *Ladies Elect*. Oxford: Oxford University Press.

Hughes, A. (1995) 'Gender and Politics in Leveller Literature', in S.D. Amussen and A.M. Kishlansky (eds) *Political Cultures and Cultural Politics in Early Modern England*. Manchester: Manchester University Press.

Hutton, O. (1992) *Woman and the Limits of Citizenship in the French Revolution*. The Donald G. Creighton Lectures 1988, Toronto: Toronto University Press.

Jacobus, M. (2001) 'Intimate Connections: Scandalous Memoirs and Epistolary Indiscretion' in E. Eger, C. Grant, C. O'Gallchoir and P. Warburton (eds) *Women, Writing and the Public Sphere*. Cambridge: Cambridge University Press: 274–80.

Kaplan, F. (2012) 'Condoleezza Rice Has a Lot of Nerve', *Slate*, 30 August, www.slate.com

Kelly, G. (1992) *Revolutionary Feminism: The Mind and Career of Mary Wollstonecraft: the Mind and Career of Mary Wollstonecraft*. New York: St Martin's Press.

Kelly, G. (1999a) *Bluestocking Feminism: Writings of the Bluestocking Circle, 1738–1785*, 6 vols, Introduction 'Bluestocking Feminism and Writing in Context'. London: Routledge.

Kelly, G. (1999b) 'Bluestocking Feminism and Writing in Context', in E. Eger (ed) *Elizabeth Montagu*, Vol 1 of 'Bluestocking Feminism: Writings of the Bluestocking Circle, 1738–1785'. London: Routledge.

Kelly, G. (2001) 'Bluestocking Feminism', in E. Eger, C. Grant, C. O'Gallchoir and P. Warburton (eds) *Women Writing and the Public Sphere, 1700–1830*. Cambridge: Cambridge University Press: 163–81.

Kelly, G. (2015) 'Bluestocking Work: Learning, Literature and Lore in the Onset of Modernity', in D. Heller (ed) *Bluestockings Now: The Evolution of a Social Role*. Farnham: Ashgate: 175–208.

Kessler, G. (2007) *The Confidante: Condoleezza Rice and the Creation of the Bush Legacy*. New York: St Martin's Press.

Klein, L. (1996) 'Coffee House Civility, 1660–1714: An Aspect of Post-courtly Culture in England', *Huntington Library Quarterly*, 59(1): 30–51.

Krugman, P. (2017) 'Elizabeth Warren on fighting for the Middle Class', Book review in *The New York Times*, May 12, www.nytimes. com

Lake, E. (2017) 'Top Obama Adviser Sought Names of Trump Associates in Intel'. *Bloomberg View*, 3 April, www.bloomberg.com

Landes, J.B. (2013) 'The Public and the Private Sphere: A Feminist Reconsideration', in J. Meehan (ed) *Feminists Read Habermas: Gendering the Subject of Discourse*. London/New York: Routledge: 91–117.

Lanser, S.S. (2003) 'Bluestocking Sapphism and the Economies of Desire', in N. Pohl and B.A. Schellenberg (eds) *Reconsidering the Bluestockings*. San Marino, CA: 257–77.

Lawrence, J. (2001) 'Contesting the Male Polity: The Suffragettes and the Politics of Disruption in Edwardian Britain' in A. Vickery (ed) *Women, Privilege and Power: British Politics 1750 to the Present*. Stanford, CA: Stanford University Press.

Lefebvre, A. and White, M. (2010) 'Mary Wollstonecraft's Civic Perfectionism', *Citizenship Studies*, 14(4), August: 461–71.

Lewis, J. (2001) '1784 and All That: Aristocratic Women and Electoral Politics', in A. Vickery (ed) *Women, Privilege and Power: British Politics 1750 to the Present*. Stanford: Stanford University Press.

Lozada, C. (2017) 'Condoleezza Rice's New Book is a Repudiation of Trump's "America First" Worldview', *The Washington Post*, May 11, www.washingtonpost.com

Mabry, M. (2007) *Twice as Good. Condoleezza and Her Path to Power*. New York: Modern Times.

Macaulay, C. (1763–83) *The History of England from the Accession of James 1 to that of the Brunswick Line*, (8 vols), London.

Macaulay, C. (1774) *A Modest Plea for the Protection of Copyright*, London and Bath: Edward and Charles Dilly.

Macaulay, C. (1790a) *Letters on Education with Observations on Religious and Metaphysical Subjects*. London.

Macaulay, C. (1790b) *Observations on the Reflections of Rt. Hon. Edmund Burke, on the Revolution in France*. London.

Mackenzie, J. (2009) 'Refiguring Universalism. Martha Nussbaum and Judith Butler – An Uneasy Alliance', *Australian Feminist Studies*, 24 (61), September: 343–58.

Mandler, P. (2001) 'From Almack's to Willis's: Aristocratic Women and Politics, 1815–67', in A. Vickery (ed) *Women, Privilege and Power: British Politics 1750 to the Present*. Stanford: Stanford University Press: 152–68.

Mann, J. (2004) *Rise of the Vulcans*. London/New York: Penguin Books.

Marcus, L. (2000) 'Woolf's Feminism and Feminism's Woolf', in S. Roe and S. Sellers (eds) *The Cambridge Companion to Virginia Woolf*. Cambridge: Cambridge University Press: 142–80.

Mead, W.R. (2017) 'America First? No, Says Former Secretary of State Condoleezza Rice', *The New York Times*, 15 May, www.nytimes.com

Meehan, J. (ed) (2013) *Feminists Read Habermas: Gendering the Subject of Discourse*. London/New York: Routledge.

Midgley, C. (2007) *Women Against Slavery: the British Campaigns, 1780–1870*. New York: Routledge.

Miller, L.B. (1996) 'Wollstonecraft, Gender Equality and the Supreme Court', in M.J. Falco (ed) *Feminist Interpretations of Mary Wollstonecraft*. Philadelphia: Pennsylvania State University Press.

Montagu, E. (1769) *An Essay on the Writings and Genius of Shakespear, Compared with the Greek and French Dramatic Poets, with Some Remarks upon the misrepresentation of Mons. De Voltaire*. London.

Montagu, E. (1810) *The letters of Mrs Elizabeth Montagu with some of the letters of her correspondents*. London: T. Cadell and W. Davies.

Montagu, E. (1825) *The letters of Mrs Elizabeth Montagu with some of the letters of her correspondents published by Matthew Montagu*. Boston: Wells and Lilly.

Montagu, E. (1974) *The letters of Mrs Elizabeth Montagu with some of the letters of her correspondents, originally published London, printed for T. Cadell and W. Davies, 1809–1813*. New York: AMS Press.

Montagu, M.W. (1716–18) [1993] *Turkish Embassy Letters*, ed A. Desai. London: William and Chatto.

Montagu Pennington, M. (ed) (1817) *Letters from Mrs Elizabeth Carter to Mrs Montagu, Between the years 1775 and 1800. Chiefly Upon Literary and Moral Subjects*, 3 vols. London.

Moore, L.L. (1997) *Dangerous Intimacies: Toward a Sapphic History of the British Novel*. Durham, NC: Duke University Press.

More, H. (1786) *Florio: A Tale of Fine Gentlemen and Fine Ladies and The Bas Bleu or Conversation, Two Poems*. London.

Morgan, S. (2007) *A Victorian Woman's Place: Public Culture in the Nineteenth Century*. New York: Palgrave, Macmillan.

Nair, P. (2013) 'Insights from Professor Warren: Analysing Elizabeth Warren's Academic Career', Bloomberg, 15 March, www.bna.com

Nava, M. (1996) 'Modernity's Disavowal: Women, the City and the Department Store', in M. Nava and A. Shea (eds) *Modern Times: Reflections on a Century of English Modernity*. London: Psychology Press: 38–50.

Nava, M. (2007) *Visceral Cosmopolitanism: Gender, Culture and the Normalisation of Difference*. Oxford: Oxford University Press.

North, A. (2013) 'The Case for Trickle Up Feminism', *Buzz Feed*, 30 January, www.buzzfeed.com

Nussbaum, M. (1999) *Sex and Social Justice*. New York: Oxford University Press.

Nussbaum, M. (2013) *Political Emotions. Why Love Matters for Justice*. Cambridge: Harvard University Press.

O'Brien, K. (2005) 'Catherine Macaulay's Histories of England: A Female Perspective on the History of Liberty', in S. Knott and B. Taylor (eds) *Women, Gender and Enlightenment*. London/New York: Palgrave, Macmillan: 523–38.

Osmos, E. (2014) 'The Samantha Power Doctrine', *The New Yorker*, 22 and 29 December, www.newyorker.com

Pateman, C. (1988) 'The Fraternal Social Contract', in J. Keane (ed) *Civil Society and the State, New European Perspectives*. London/New York: Verso: 101–29.

Pateman, C. (1989) 'Feminist Critiques of the Public/Private Dichotomy', in *The Disorder of Women: Democracy, Feminism and Political Theory*. Cambridge: Polity Press: 118–41.

Peltz, L. (2008) 'A Revolution in Female Manners' in E. Eger and L. Peltz *Brilliant Women: 18th Century Bluestockings*. London: National Portrait Gallery: 94–126.

Philips, A. (2001) 'Feminism and Liberalism Revisited. Has Martha Nussbaum Got it Right?', *Constellations*, 8 (2): 249–66.

Piozzi, H.L. (1786) 'Anecdotes of the Late Samuel Johnson', in A. Sherbo (ed) *Memoirs of the Life and Writings of the Late Samuel Johnson*. London.

Pohl, N. (2015) 'Cosmopolitan Bluestockings', in D. Heller (ed) *Bluestockings Now: The Evolution of a Social Role*. Farnham: Ashgate: 71–91.

Pohl, N. and Schellenberg, B.A. (eds) (2003) *Reconsidering the Bluestockings*. San Marino, CA: Huntington Library.

Polwhele, R. ([1798] 1974) *The Unsex'd Females: A Poem [by] Richard Polwhele*. New York: Garland Publishing.

Porter, R. (2004) *Flesh in the Age of Reason: The Modern Foundations of Body and Soul*. New York: W.W. Norton.

Potts, M. (2015) 'Why Do Feminists Hate Sheryl Sandberg So Much?', *The Daily Beast*, 3 December 2015, www.thedailybeast.com

Power, S. (2002) 'Raising the Cost of Genocide', *Dissent*, 49(2), 1 April.

Power, S. (2003) *'A Problem from Hell': America and the Age of Genocide*. New York: Hachette Books.

Power, S. (2004a) 'Introduction' to *Hannah Arendt: The Origins of Totalitarianis*. New York: Penguin/Random House.

Power, S. (2004b) 'Reporting Neutrality: War, Atrocities and the Danger of Taking Sides', *International Journal of Press/Politics*, 9(3), 1 July: 3–11.

Power, S. (2005) 'Dying in Dafur' in American Society of Magazine Editors *The Best American Magazine Writing*. Columbia University Press.

Power, S. (2008a) *Chasing the Flame: Sergio Vieirade Mello and the Fight to Save the World*. London: Allen Lane/Penguin Books.

Power, S. (2008b) '"Stopping Genocide and Securing Justice": Learning by Doing – International Justice, War Crimes, and Terrorism: The US Record' in R. Fall, H. Elder and K. Hajjor (eds) *Human Rights: Critical Concepts in Political Science 274*, New York: Routledge.

Power, S. (2008c) 'The United States and the Genocide Law: A History of Ambivalence' in A. Jones (ed) *Genocide*, vol 4, London: Sage.

Power, S. and Chollett, D. (eds) (2011) *The Unquiet American: Richard Holbrooke in the World*. New York: Public Affairs.

Price, J., Ditchfield, G.M. and Lucas, B. (1991) *A Kentish Parson: Selections from the Private Papers of the Revd Joseph Price, Vicar of Brabourne, 1767–1786*. Maidstone: Kent County Council Arts and Libraries.

Rendall, J. (1985) *The Origins of Modern Feminism*. Basingstoke: Palgrave.

Reynolds, K.D. (1998) *Aristocratic Women and Political Society in Victorian Britain*. Oxford: Oxford University Press.

Rice, C. (2000) 'Promoting the National Interest', *Foreign Affairs*, 79(1), Jan/Feb: 45–62.

Rice, C. (2008) 'Rethinking the National Interest: American Realism for a New World', *Foreign Affairs*, 87(4), July/Aug: 2–26.

Rice, C. (2010) *Extraordinary Ordinary People: A Memoir of Family*. New York: Random House.

Rice, C. (2011) *No Higher Honor: A Memoir of My Years in Washington*. New York: Crown Publishers.

Rice, C. (2017) *Democracy: Stories from the Long Road to Freedom*. New York: Grand Central Publishing.

Robins, E. (1907 [1980]) *The Convert*. New York: Feminist Press: City University of New York.

Rhys, J. (1966) *Wide Sargasso Sea*. Andre Deutsch (UK)/W.W. Norton (US).

Roberts, W. (1834) 'Letter from Hannah More to one of Her Sisters' in *Memoirs of the Life and Correspondence of Mrs Hannah More*, 4 vols, London.

Sandberg, S. (2013) *Lean In: Women, Work and the Will to Lead*. New York: Knopf.

Sapiro, V. (1992) *A Vindication of Political Virtue: The Political Theory of Mary Wollstonecraft*. Chicago: University of Chicago Press.

Schwoerer, L. (1998) 'Women's Public Political Voice in England, 1640–1740', in H. Smith (ed) *Women Writers and the Early Modern British Political Tradition*. Cambridge: Cambridge University Press: 56–75.

Scott, S. (1762) *A Description of Millenium Hall and the Country Adjacent*, ed G. Kelly, London.

Scott, W.S. (1947) *The Bluestocking Ladies*, London: John Green & Co.

Skinner, K.K., Kudelia, S., De Mesquita, B. and Rice, C. (2007) *The Strategy of Campaigning*. Ann Arbor, MI: University of Michigan Press.

Slaughter, A.M. (2012) 'Why Women Still Can't Have It All', *The Atlantic*, July/August:1–42.

Smith, D. (2017) 'Here Comes Hillary Clinton's Memoir and There's Plenty of Blame to Go Round', *Guardian*, 8 September, www.theguardian.com

Smith, H. (ed) (1998) *Women Writers and the Early Modern British Political Tradition*. Cambridge: Cambridge University Press.

Sommers, C.H. (2013) 'What "Lean In" Misunderstands About Gender Differences', *The Atlantic*, 19 March, www.theatlantic.com

Sorkin, A.D. (2012) 'The Impossible Condoleezza Rice', *The New Yorker*, 30 August, www.newyorker.com

Stetson-McBridge, D. (1996) 'Women's Rights and Human Rights: Intersection and Conflict', in M.J. Falco (ed) *Feminist Interpretations of Mary Wollstonecraft*. Philadelphia: Pennsylvania State University Press: 165–79.

Stowe, H.B. (1852) *Uncle Tom's Cabin*. Boston: Jewett, Proctor & Worthington.

Taylor, B. (1993) *Wollstonecraft and the Feminist Imagination*. Cambridge: Cambridge University Press.

Taylor, B. (2005) 'Feminists versus Gallants: Sexual Manners and Morals in Enlightenment Britain', in S. Knott and B. Taylor (eds) *Women, Gender and Enlightenment*. Basingstoke: Palgrave, Macmillan: 30–53.

Todd, J. and Butler, M. (eds) (1989) *The Works of Mary Wollstonecraft*, V (7 vols). London: William Pickering.

Traister, R. (2016) 'Hillary Clinton vs Herself', *New Yorker Magazine*, May 30, www.nymag.com

Valenti, J. (2013) 'Sheryl Sandberg Isn't the Perfect Feminist. So What?', *The Washington Post*, 1 March, www.washingtonpost.com

Vickery, A. (ed) (2001) *Women, Privilege and Power: British Politics 1750 to the Present*. Stanford: Stanford University Press.

Warren, E. (2017) *This Fight is Our Fight: The Battle to Save America's Middle-Class*. New York: Metropolitan Books.

Williams, Z. (2013) 'Lean In: Women, Work and the Will to Lead', *Guardian*, 13 March, www.theguardian.com

Wiseman, S. (2001) 'Catherine Macaulay: History, Republicanism and the Public Sphere', in E. Eger, C. Grant, C. O'Gallchoir and P. Warburton (eds) *Women, Writing and the Public Sphere, 1700–1830*. Cambridge: Cambridge University Press: 181–99.

Wolfson, C. (2008) 'The Legacy of Condoleezza Rice', *CBS News*, 19 December, www.cbsnews.com

Wollstonecraft, M. (1787) *Thoughts on the Education of Daughters: with Reflections on Female Conduct in the More Important Duties of Life*. London: J. Johnson.

Wollstonecraft, M. (1788 [1989]) 'Mary: A Fiction' in M. Butler and J. Todd (eds), *The Works of Mary Wollstonecraft*, vol 1. London: Pickering and Chatto.

Wollstonecraft, M. (1792a) *A Vindication of the Rights of Woman*. London.

Wollstonecraft, M. (1792b [1988]) *A Vindication of the Rights of Woman*, ed. C.H. Poston. New York: Norton.

Wollstonecraft, M. (1794 [1989]) 'An Historical and Moral View of the Origin and Progress of the French Revolution and the Effects it has Produced on Europe' in M. Butler and J. Todd (eds) *The Works of Mary Wollstonecraft*. London: Pickering and Chatto.

Wollstonecraft, M. (1798 [1989]) 'Maria, or The Wrongs of Woman', in M. Butler and J. Todd (eds) *The Works of Mary Wollstonecraft*. London: Pickering and Chatto.

Wollstonecraft, M. (1790 [1994]) 'A Vindication of the Rights of Men', in J. Todd (ed) *Mary Wollstonecraft Political Writings*. Oxford: Oxford University Press.

Wollstonecraft, M. (1792 [1994]) 'A Vindication of the Rights of Woman' in J. Todd (ed) *Mary Wollstonecraft Political Writings*. Oxford: Oxford University Press.

Wollstonecraft, M. (1996) *A Vindication of the Rights of Men and a Vindication of the Rights of Woman*. Cambridge: Cambridge University Press.

Zelikow, P. and Rice, C. (1995) *Germany Unified and Europe Transformed*. Harvard, MA: Harvard University Press.

Zenko, M. (2011) 'City of Men', *Foreign Policy*, 14 July, www.bna.com

Zenko, M. (2012) 'Ask the Experts: Where Are the Women in Foreign Policy?', *Council on Foreign Relations*, 8 March, www.cfr.org

Zilber, A. (2017) 'Controversial Feminist, Camille Paglia Slams "Insufferably Smug and Entitled" Facebook CEO, Sheryl Sandberg for "Hiding Her Servants and Nannies"', *Daily Mail*, 15 March, www.dailymail.com.uk

Index

Morgan, S. 72
motherhood *see* family life and work-
life balance
MSNBC 125

N

Nair, P. 112, 113
Nation, The 116
National Union of Women's Suffrage
Societies (NUWSS) 76
National Women's Liberation
Movement Conference (1970) 78
Nava, M. 75
New Republic, The 117
'New Woman' 67, 76, 135, 137
New York Times, The 80, 87, 112, 114,
118
New Yorker, The 116–17
North, A. 117
North Korea 89–90
Northanger Abbey (Austen) 54–5, 63
Nussbaum, M. 20–1, 131

O

Obama, Barack 85, 92–5, 97, 98,
99–103, 124–5
O'Brien, K. 36, 41, 133
*Observations on the Reflections of the Rt.
Hon. Edmund Burke on the Revolution
in France* (Macaulay) 42, 43, 61
Osmos, E. 90, 91–7, 101

P

Paglia, Camille 117
Pankhurst, Emmeline 76
parenthood *see* family life and work-
life balance
Parkes, Bessie Rayner 73, 74
party politics 69–70, 76–7
Pateman, C. 16, 21, 28, 131
patriotism 10, 14, 41
Peltz, L. ix, 1, 2, 23–4, 33, 35–6, 46–7,
60–1
Pennington, Sarah 53–4
Perez, Martin 92
Persuasion (Austen) 54–5
philanthropy 75–6, 136
Philips, A. 20–1
Piozzi, Gabriel 4, 54
Piozzi, Hester Lynch Thrale 3, 4, 10,
22, 51, 54
Pohl, N. ix, xiv, 1, 2, 3–4, 9–10, 12,
13–14
political parties 69–70, 76–7
Politico Magazine 84, 87
politics
and aristocratic women 68, 69–70
and bluestockings x, xi, 3–10, 13, 45

early involvement in 68–9
electioneering 68, 69–70
and Macaulay, Elizabeth xi, 23–4,
35–41, 43–6, 61
party politics 69–70, 76–7
and print culture 68–9, 70–1, 136
and public sphere 13–22
republicanism 36, 39, 41, 61
violence at meetings 77, 137
and Wollstonecraft, Mary 23–4,
26–32, 33–4, 44–5, 58–9
and Woolf, Virginia 64
see also social movements; suffrage;
United States
Pollitt, Kate 116
Polwhele, Richard 60–1
Unsex'd Females, The 60
Porter, Jane 65
Porter, R. xii, 24
Potts, M. 116–17, 118–19
poverty 43–4, 44–5
Power, Samantha 90–7
academic career 91–2
contribution and legacy 96–7
early years 90–1
*Problem from Hell: America and the Age
of Genocide* 91–2
publications of 91–2, 95–6
and Rice, Susan 94
service to the administration 92–5
Pride and Prejudice (Austen) 54–5
print culture 68–9, 70–1
*Problem from Hell: America and the Age of
Genocide* (Power) 91–2
professionalization 18, 57, 58, 62, 63,
75, 134
professions, access to 27, 74
property ownership 15, 17, 30, 43–4,
75
pseudonyms 61
public intellectualism
bluestockings 7–11
broadening role of women 75–6
emerging women intellectuals 21–2,
131
and philanthropy 75–6
and print culture 68–9, 70–1
see also social movements; United
States; women writers
public sphere x–xi, 13–22, 130–1
emerging women intellectuals 21–2
and feminism 16–19, 130
and gender 13–14, 17–21, 71–2,
130–1
and Habermas, J. 13–14, 15–20, 71,
130–1
as intermediary space 16–20
and philanthropy 75–6